Teaching and Learning Languages

Learning a language, especially in a class or group, is an intensely practical subject. Active participation by students is the key to successful language learning at any age or ability level. This book offers teachers a multitude of practical activities in which students take the lead, and clearly links these to the various linguistic and pragmatic skills.

The book provides clear and comprehensive guidance on the classroom environment, models of teaching and learning, and assessment. It aims to help teachers plan engaging lessons that will enable all students to develop the key skills of speaking, listening, reading and writing in the target language. Topics covered include:

- The essentials of language learning
- Use of the target language; training the ear and training the voice
- Exploiting audio and video recordings
- Exploiting texts and pictures
- Using stories and drama in the classroom, and independent reading
- Making good use of written work
- Integrating multimedia resources and the Internet across the language skills
- Integrating grammar into communication.

Teaching and Learning Languages has been written in line with national and European language policies, reflecting contemporary trends in the teaching and learning of languages. The text's focus on active learning and its indispensable guidance for planning lessons make it essential reading for all trainee and practising teachers.

Jemma Buck taught in British secondary schools for 10 years, where she was involved in continuing language learning, in-service teacher training and writing textbooks. She now works as a *Maître de Conférences* (Lecturer) in Second Language Acquisition at the University of Nantes, France.

Christopher Wightwick taught languages for 25 years before becoming an HMI, finishing as Staff Inspector for Modern Foreign Languages. He has written a three-volume German course and a German grammar handbook. He is now an educational consultant and is the general editor for the Berlitz Language Handbooks.

Teaching and Learning Languages

A practical guide to learning by doing

Jemma Buck and
Christopher Wightwick

Routledge
Taylor & Francis Group

LONDON AND NEW YORK

First published 2013
by Routledge
2 Park Square, Milton Park, Abingdon, Oxon OX14 4RN

Simultaneously published in the USA and Canada
by Routledge
711 Third Avenue, New York, NY 10017

Routledge is an imprint of the Taylor & Francis Group, an informa business

British Library Cataloguing in Publication Data
A catalogue record for this book is available from the British Library

Library of Congress Cataloging in Publication Data
 Buck, Jemma.
 Teaching and learning languages: a practical guide to learning by doing / Jemma Buck and
 Christopher Wightwick.
   p. cm.
 ISBN 978-0-415-63839-5 — ISBN 978-0-415-63840-1 (pbk.) — ISBN 978-0-203-08242-3
 (ebook) 1. Language and languages—Study and teaching.   2. Group work in education.
 I. Wightwick, Christopher.   II. Title.
 P53.42.B74 2012
 418.0071—dc23   2012022398

ISBN: 978-0-415-63839-5 (hbk)
ISBN: 978-0-415-63840-1 (pbk)
ISBN: 978-0-203-08242-3 (ebk)

Typeset in Celeste
by RefineCatch Limited, Bungay, Suffolk

Printed and bound in Great Britain by the MPG Books Group

Contents

Contents

Contents

Figures and Tables

Figures

Table

Preface

At a time when funding is short and the market offers many works on the teaching of modern foreign languages (MFL), it is fair to ask: "Why another book? What's it for?" In a nutshell, this book explores ways by which you, the teacher, can enable students to participate to the maximum in their own learning. Naturally, we discuss various other topics that influence "learning by doing", but the concentration on this central theme, we believe, distinguishes the book from all others.

The contents have been gathered from a wide variety of sources: classroom observation, conferences, books and elsewhere. A good number originated in two of the Teachers' Books of a proposed French course; the originals were produced by the two present authors and Kate Beeching, Reader in French and Linguistics at the University of the West of England, to whom we owe especial thanks. Other sources are acknowledged in the text.

In some chapters, the suggestions made are illustrated by boxed examples. These examples are not meant to be the only way to do things, nor are they class exercises; they are simply intended to clarify the text and to provide some new ideas. They are given in English, French, German or Spanish, but the principles apply to all languages. (We realise that you may not be fluent in all these languages, but we didn't want one language to dominate, and we believe that the way the examples are laid out gives a good idea of their purpose, even without full comprehension.) We are very grateful to Jane Gaafar (www.g-and-w. co.uk) for recommending that these examples be included, as well as for other timely help.

To ensure that the text reflects best practice and relates fully to the National Curriculum for Secondary Schools and the Key Stage 3 Framework for Modern Foreign Languages, and thus serves the needs of teachers, it has been thoroughly revised by Neil Jones, Assistant Headteacher, Sir John Cass Redcoat School, Stepney, London. We are very grateful for his meticulous work and incisive contributions.

We owe grateful thanks to all those who have scrutinised our work and made useful suggestions. They include: the Strubelt family of Bremen, for their comments on the German-language boxes; students of Nantes University for their valuable discussions; and especially Vanessa Taunay and Kadija El Boazzati for their help with the Spanish.

Finally, we greatly appreciate the support and guidance given us throughout by Annamarie Kino-Wylam, Commissioning Editor at Routledge, and in the finishing stages by Natalie Meylan and other members of the Routledge team. This greatly improved the coherence of the book.

THREE AXIOMS

To teach = to enable learning

Learning comes best through doing

"Answering teachers' questions isn't *doing* anything"[1]

---

[1]   A remark made by a student during a survey by HMI.

The essentials of language learning

Reading maketh a full man, conference a ready man, and writing an exact man.

(Francis Bacon, *Of Studies*, 1625)

However carefully planned, if a lesson centres on the teacher for too long, students lose the chance to use what they know. This in turn leads to disenchantment with the subject and reluctance to go on doing it. The inclusion of a language as a core subject in the English Baccalaureate should provide a strong incentive to remedy this situation. However, in the absence of reflection on the central problem of too much teacher-talk, to the detriment of students' action, any increased uptake is more likely to result from necessity than from real interest in the subject. That is the problem that we seek to tackle in this book. Language-learning research has seen a marked shift in recent years, from a teacher-centred to a learner-centred and now to a learning-centred approach – that we interpret as an approach to teaching and learning that places maximum emphasis on students' full participation in every activity.

Language learning has a lot in common with craft design technology (CDT): in both, students must develop a firm understanding of basic principles, but the purpose of the whole thing is "doing" – applying knowledge in practical activities. In languages, "doing" means communicating, "Applying linguistic knowledge and skills to understand and communicate effectively".[1] This includes reading and writing, and Chapters 15 to 18 explore ways of using these, but in the classroom communication mainly means talking to fellow-students – "interacting". Putting such activities at the centre of planning is the key to successful and enjoyable lessons, so the major part of the book (Chapters 7 to 14) concentrates on classroom activities that promote at least partly sponta-neous talk.

---

[1] Modern Foreign Languages Programme of Study: key stage 3 (2008) §1.1b.

Essentials of language learning

The Common European Framework (CEF) promotes the use of learning through doing:

> The approach adopted here ... is an action-oriented one in so far as it views users and learners of a language primarily as 'social agents', i.e. members of a society who have tasks (not exclusively language related) to accomplish in a given set of circumstances, in a specific environment and within a particular field of action.[2]
>
> (CEF, section 2.1, p. 9)

For the CEF, "tasks" are defined as: "actions performed by one or more individuals strategically using their own specific competences to achieve a given result" (ibid.). Such collaborative activities engage students actively in their own learning and help them to develop general skills such as the ability to organise their work, to work by themselves and with others, and to become self-confident in their use of the target language. Furthermore, they correspond neatly to the idea of learning-centred approaches, which is also at the base of three important aims of language learning that are met throughout this book. These are as follows.

- *Intercultural understanding*: Throughout the book, but especially in Chapters 9 to 18, there are many opportunities to enhance students' understanding of life as it is lived in the country of the target language, through activities as varied as studying advertisements, planning projects and exploring encyclopaedias. Any authentic input is likely to be loaded with intercultural awareness. This is precisely because it is difficult to divorce the language from the culture, and the language is an entrance to the culture.

- *Thinking skills*: Chapter 20 lists four specific examples, but numerous other activities require considerable individual or cooperative thought.

- *Language learning strategies*: Similarly, Chapters 15 (on reading), 19 (on vocabulary and phraseology) and 20 (on grammar) comment specifically on how students learn, but many others require them to put their strategies into action.

Though apparently distinct, these aspects of language learning have in common that all three are dependent on students' active participation in the activities they undertake, and while they can't be taught in any formal way, they can be discussed and experimented with. Encouraging reflection on how to learn a word is focusing on strategies for acquiring vocabulary. Discussing how to understand a new word from context involves recognising strategy.

No linguistic task can be carried out without an ever-increasing fund of language, and that goes for all the activities suggested here. One of the best sources of language is independent reading, but words and phrases have to be

---

[2] www.coe.int/t/dg4/linguistic/Source/Framework_EN.pdf

systematically learnt before they can be used, so this topic is treated at some length in Chapter 19.

What, though, of the basic principles – the understanding of the structures of the language? Understanding and being able to apply "the underlying model" can mean the difference between partial or phrasebook communication and nuanced communication. Although the general teaching of grammar is far too complex a subject to be dealt with fully here, the Chapter 20 of the book deals with possible steps towards mastering the underlying model – "Understanding how a language works and how to manipulate it"[3] – and suggests some related tasks. Throughout the book, many of the activities are in fact based on the relationship between communication and structure, which can be made more or less explicit as required. Interestingly, the cognitive approach to language learning is evoked many times in the CEF, reflecting current research in second-language acquisition, particularly in its importance in developing life-long language-learning strategies.

This book naturally concentrates on particular activities, but these will take place in very different environments. Our second chapter therefore considers the physical setting of the classroom and suggests ways of arranging it so as to help you set up these activities. Chapters 3 and 4 then look at aspects of lesson planning and of assessment, before Chapter 5 returns to the main subject of the book.

The later chapters contain a multitude of suggested activities, and we are well aware that this can appear rather overwhelming – you could suffer from *un embarras de choix*. We appreciate, too, that you are likely to be following a published course book, where the exercises may well not follow the same principles as we do. For this reason we have as far as possible grouped activities together, for example into those showing use of audio-visual resources, or vocabulary and phraseology, or grammatical constructions. You could home in on one of the chapters with most activities, trying them out for a while with any suitable class and topic. Even if you pick an activity almost at random, you should find it quite easy to slant it to support your current objectives. We hope, too, that as you get to know the book better you will recognise that certain exercises fit well with certain topics.

At various places in the text we quote from the 2008 *Modern Foreign Languages Programme of Study* for Key Stage 3, the crucial link between Key Stage 2 MFL and the examination years. But this does not mean that the approach we recommend is suitable for these years only, important though they are. Active learning is the key to success at any age, so we seldom suggest suitable age- or ability-levels; most activities can be made harder or easier to suit the class.

To sum up: this book is not wedded to any hard-and-fast "method". At different stages, you could place more emphasis on, say, oral work, grammatical structures

---

[3] Ibid, §1.2a.

or vocabulary/phrase-building, so long as it results in students' learning to use the language and understand how it works. At its core, the book is a compendium of practical activities designed to help this happen. It does not claim to be thoroughly original: indeed, some of the activities suggested are old favourites, and may even remind you of grandmothers sucking eggs. Other suggestions are perhaps more novel, and a few may appear impossibly difficult "for my class". Because language cannot be divided into completely separate compartments, some suggestions appear in more than one chapter. But all have the same aim, namely, to provide you with some ideas that you might not otherwise have thought of, and above all to enable students to play a really active role in their own learning. Suggestions that are successful for one teacher or for one class may be less successful for others. We can only say:

Try it, adapt it if it doesn't work, postpone it if it still doesn't. Remember, though, that

ALL STUDENTS NEED TRAINING IN NEW WAYS OF WORKING, AND THE
EARLIER THE BETTER.

CHAPTER 2

The classroom environment

The purpose of this book is to suggest strategies to promote students' active participation in their own learning, mainly through cooperative work. But experience shows that even the best-laid plans can be thwarted by the layout of the classroom. You can set up a carousel of activities (see later in this chapter) – problem solved. But not every room is suitable for carousels, so (at the risk of pointing out the obvious) this chapter begins by suggesting ways of setting up your room to enable students to work together.

Arranging the seating

Classrooms come in all shapes and sizes. They also exist within external constraints, such as the ban on moving any furniture on pain of being ostracised by the caretaker staff! If you are lucky enough to have free rein on designing your own arrangements, then you might consider those outlined in Table 2.1.

Table 2.1 Seating arrangements

Design	Advantages	Disadvantages	Uses
U-shaped – all tables placed so as to form a U. Your own desk can be placed to one side to allow clear vision of the board, or centre front, or central, to allow you a clearer influence on what happens. If you break the U in the corners (like a digital U), access is made even easier.	Easy access to all students at all times. Central space available to be used for drama, or any other activity. Students turn to or away from their partners for pair-work. Alternate pairs move their chairs to the other side of their neighbours' table for group-work.	Doesn't lend itself easily to group-work. Demands a lot of space, a large classroom. Teacher tends to be distant from the action, so can lead to frontal teaching techniques. This is especially so if the teacher's table is central and at the front as s/he becomes the focal point of the room.	Pair-work, individual study, monologue or small group presentations, drama. Whole-class mingling activities are easy to promote in the central space.

(Continued overleaf)

Table 2.1 Continued

Design	Advantages	Disadvantages	Uses
Double U-shaped – tables arranged to form a double U. Your table as above.	Easier to organise pair-work and small group work. Easy access to front row of students.	Back row corners can become totally inaccessible. For this reason alone can be a difficult shape to use.	As above.
As above (either single or double U) but with a central set of work tables. Your table can be part of the central set, or to one side.	As above, easy access to students. Can be good for group-work. Above all, the digital U with a central set of tables makes it easy to organise carousel lessons. In this case, this central set can be the space designated for accessing teacher help or for teacher-led remedial work.	Less room for drama, mingling, etc.	Carousel work, individual work, small-group work.
Daisy-shaped – groups of two/three double or five/six single tables together.	Wonderful for small-group work, collaborative projects, cooperative writing tasks, etc.	Some students will develop cricked necks as they have to turn around to see what's on the board.	Group-work, carousel work.
Fixed rows – either in long rows or separate tables.	Easy access to all students, less easy if the rows are long. Encourages a degree of formality and seriousness in the classroom.	Difficult to reorganise for group-work, mingling, drama, etc. In long rows, difficult to get to all students, so can encourage lack of participation.	Formal assessment. Whole-class sessions. Pairs/groups can be formed if every other row turns round to face the row behind.
Designated spaces (a reading corner, a writing area, an ICT area, a listening area, a structures area, a speaking area, all equipped for the specific purpose).	Perfect for carousel working. Usually leaves a space for mingling etc.	Hard to use for other activities.	Carousel and mingling/drama.

Setting up pair-work

(See also Chapters 7 and 8.) Working in pairs usually requires less rearrangement of seating than working in groups, though even here two things are worth considering.

- Should pairs be of equal ability, or is it sometimes better for a more advanced student to partner one less advanced? If the latter, the stronger student can provide very useful guidance, but care must be taken not to create a sense of inferiority in the weaker member.

- How well do the members of the pair know each other? If the exercise requires each to find out things about the other, then it may be better for them not to be "best friends".

As both these arrangements may involve changing the seating, it helps to give each student a personal number. Seating plans can then be displayed, e.g. on an OHP or whiteboard. Another way of setting up new pairs is for students to draw lots. Half the students put their numbers into a box and the other half draw their partners' numbers.

Some exercises require students to move, which may mean changing partners in an ordered sequence (e.g., "Multiple partners" in Chapter 8), or full-scale "milling", where students move freely from one partner to the next, asking questions. In both cases, make sure that the direction of travel is clear to all students. Control the extent of the movement by forming separate smaller clusters, and have clear signals for start and finish.

Setting up group-work

(See also Chapter 9.) Small groups (i.e. three to five) are usually the best setting for students to interact. They also make it much easier for the majority to get on with the task, and more difficult for the less industrious to be a nuisance. In addition, as you move round the class, small groups are the ideal setting for you to forge relationships with students and monitor their progress.

If your classroom is set up in rows, get every other row to turn round to face the row behind; it is then easy to make groups of three or four. Small groups can easily be combined to form larger groups if needed, for example for drama (see Chapter 12).

Carousel working

In carousel working, different areas of the room are set up for different activities. Carousels can be theme-based (all the activities revolve around a central theme, with specific activities to practise all the skills) or can be revision-based (with banks of activities that the student dips into). A certain degree of guided autonomy is promoted by the former, but there is a greater degree of autonomy in the latter.

Carousels can be used to focus on learning strategies, either through a plenary session focusing on the strategies the students used to accomplish the task, or with a specific focus on strategies as part of each activity; both enable students to voice their opinions. Carousels can also be used as an assessment tool, and any additional staffing such as foreign language assistants can play an integral part in the lesson and assessment processes. In particular, carousels can be very successful in promoting the assessment of individual speech or small-group interaction.

Carousel lessons are also useful for enabling differentiation. Each area of the carousel can be considered as a skills workshop, and the banks of activities can be classified by level, so that the students can decide at what level they wish to work. The level can be adjusted according to input (the level of the text that is being worked on) or to output (the kind of activity that is required). The activities should include a separate answer "key" and, in the case of the speaking activities, the ability to record the performance. Students can then work at the level they choose, and self-assess the answers. Or, if the students are working in pairs or small groups, they can peer-assess.

Some of the following suggestions would be worth a try.

- *Listening stations.* Benches facing the wall to promote concentration; CD/DVD/MP3 players with single and multiple outlets and headphones; stocks of listening material, listed for speedy access.

- *Video.* If it can be done without disturbing others, groups of three or four can work together on short video sequences, perhaps with each member taking it in turn to be "in charge".

- *Drama and role-play.* An area allowing movement and some use of props, away from the quiet areas. With some groups, an area outside the classroom can be used.

- *Group discussion, games, etc.* Chairs grouped round a table, with sufficient clear space to lay out material.

- *Reading.* A quiet corner with carpet, comfortable seating and a range of dictionaries and other reference works, as well as opportunities for reading fiction and magazines for pleasure.

- *Writing.* For extended writing by individuals or small groups. Benches facing the wall, suitable writing surfaces, a shelf of catalogued reference materials.

- *ICT.* Stand-alone or networked machines, away from the quiet areas so that two or three students can work together; clear instructions and ICT-specific vocabulary in the target language on display.

- *Tutorial.* For you to work with selected groups of students.

We trust that the suggestions in this chapter provide useful guidance on possible ways to set up your classroom. There are, of course, as many ways as there are classrooms, but in approaching this problem, remember that the essential is to start with how you wish to structure your lessons and then to work, as far as you can, to ensure that your classroom layout helps rather than hinders you.

CHAPTER 3

Some teaching and learning modes

There are many ways to run a lesson. In this book, we will develop these in more detail, with chapters dedicated to group-work, pair-work and individual action-based work. This chapter, by contrast, focuses more on whole-class or plenary sessions.

Plenary sessions can be used within an action-based approach as part of a pre-task for:

- the introduction and instructions for a project, before dispersal into smaller units
- brainstorming
- pre-listening
- anticipation.

Plenary sessions can be used within an action-based approach as part of a post-task for:

- a focus on form (see Chapter 20)
- a focus on vocabulary
- groups to report back to other groups, to present their projects, their drama, etc.

Every class has its own characteristics. The following two patterns illustrate opposite ends of the range, but each contains elements present in most lessons.

Two contrasting lesson patterns

- *The diamond-shaped lesson plan*: starting a lesson with a quiet activity for a boisterous class, followed by a noisier/more active activity and then reverting to a quiet closing activity.
- *The X-shaped lesson plan*: conversely, with a very quiet class, starting and ending with a bang, with a more reflective activity in the middle.

In this way, the students are led to explore activities out of their comfort zone but still have some class periods that are more suited to their temperament. They also receive a clear message that you are directing the class, an especially important message in the more active parts.

The elements of these lessons include the following.

- Input and questioning led by you, setting a process in motion, not too lengthily. The main aim of such a session will be to concentrate attention on what the class has learnt or is about to learn, and your questions check and reinforce understanding.

- Reversing this, students ask you questions either of a general nature (can be risky!) or about a recently studied image, text or topic – you are not allowed to look at the text while answering. This exercise is valuable both as a check on learning, in that no-one can ask a question about something they haven't read, and as a means of allowing students to take some control of the activity. It is also self-differentiating – the type (or even absence) of questions asked tells you a lot about who has understood what.

- Pairs, "milling" (moving about the classroom asking questions) and other forms of intensive oral practice, perhaps linked to writing. Pair-work is dealt with extensively in Chapter 8. "Milling" can appear to be an invitation to chaos, which can best be controlled by breaking up the class into its "larger groups", but the chief risk is that students do not stick to the target language. Both the successful use of groups and knowledge of questioning language depend on thorough preparation and regular training.

- Shorter or longer bouts of small-group work, linked to the current class activity but extending it in directions that may not be wholly foreseeable. (See Chapter 9.)

- Improvised drama, where students can use the target language with some degree of spontaneity. (See Chapter 12.)

- Carousels, with different activities set up at various points in the room (see above).

- Sessions of silent reading, which could be just a re-reading of an already studied text or, preferably, a different text in a similar situation, providing reinforcement of vocabulary and phraseology.

- Individual written work, either in class or for homework, using the notes students have made during group sessions. (See Chapter 17.)

A *diamond-shaped lesson* might go as follows, possibly across more than one session.

i. A period of silent reading, followed by questions from the teacher.

Teaching and learning modes

Por ejemplo . . .   *UNA CLASE . . . EN FORMA DE ROMBO*

Profe: ¡Buenos días todos! Para empezar, vosotros van a leer de nuevo la pequeña historia que hemos estudiado ayer – la he puesto sobre la pizarra blanca. Tenéis 5 minutos . . . !No necesitas discutir Jean! . . . Bueno, cerrad vuestros libros. Dígame, Elodie, ¿dónde ocurre la historia? . . . Hassan, ¿a qué hora el desconocido llega? . . .

---

ii. Students ask the teacher questions.

Profe: Bueno, ahora vosotros van a preguntarme cuestiones sobre la historia. Cerro mi libro. Si, Théo.

Théo: ¿Donde vive la familia Lebrun?

Profe: En Bordeaux.

Théo: Si, pero ¿donde en Bordeaux?

Profe: No se – ¿en el centro de la cuidad?

Théo: ¡No! ¡En un barrio! Un punto menos Señora.

---

iii. "Milling" in larger groups. Assumed here that the class has long experience of working in larger/smaller groups.

Profe: Vale, ¡levantaos todos, y formad vuestro grupo de seis o siete! Circulad en vuestros grupos y haced unos y otros preguntas sobre la historia. Yo también, voy a circular. Tenéis 5 minutos. ¡Pero hacedlo tranquilo!

---

iv. Working in smaller groups, students elaborate on the original story.

Profe: Bien, bien. Tenéis buenas preguntas. ¡Sentaos! Ahora, haced vuestros grupos de tres o cuatro. El desconocido llega al fin de la historia. ¿Qué quiere? ¿Y qué ocurre? Discutid en vuestros grupos, inventad, haced notas de vuestra conclusión. Os doy 10 minutos.

---

v. To conclude the activity, students could:

- take it in turns to narrate their version of the story to the class
- write up the newly extended story, having chosen one of the group to act as scribe
- (if necessary in larger groups, partly as homework) rework the story as a drama, each member taking a specific role both in the writing and in the

performance. This is by some way the most demanding task, but a suitable challenge for older students. (See Chapter 17.)

An *X-shaped lesson* might go as follows, possibly across more than one session.

i. You choose in advance the theme of the session(s) and prepare a quick mutual dictation on the theme, which will provoke discussion and will give some essential vocabulary. Here, we've chosen public transport. (Dictation with blanks: see Chapter 8, "Fixed partners".)

Por ejemplo . . .   *UNA CLASE EN FORMA DE X . . .*

Profe: ¡Buenos días todos! Vamos a empezar hoy con un dictado entre dos. Poneos en pares. Luego, poneos espalda contra espalda. Las personas A – esté es vuestra partida del texto con los blancos. Y esté el texto de las personas B (*mostrar la actividad con un retroproyector.*) ¿Sabéis la reglas del juego, no? Sí, es eso, la persona A empieza dictando su primera parte de frase, y la persona B escribe lo que entiende. Luego, es la persona B quien dicta y la persona A que escribe. Y seguimos de la misma manera hasta el final. ¿Preguntas? ¿No? Muy bien – ¡Empezad! . . .

Ahora, comparad vuestros textos y recoged los partes donde había problemas. Intentad identificar porqué eso fue un problema.

---

ii. Students reflect in pairs as to the problems they had (quiet activity). They then ask you questions about the new vocabulary and also about the theme. You will already have prepared ways of helping them understand.

Profe: Estoy segura que hay palabras desconocidas en este texto – ¿Quíen puedo identificarlos?

Debbie: No entiendo "embotellamiento".

Profe: ¿Alguien puede ayudarla?

Martin: Sé que "botella", eso quiere decir "bottle", pero . . .

Profe: Muy bien, verdad, eso os da una idea . . .

Freya: Pero el texto, el tema claro, es el autobús, los tranvías, los trenes . . .

Profe: Hay una frase en el texto que reúne todos estos medios de transporte. ¿Quién le ha encontrado?

Lily: ¿Transporte en común?

Profe: Sí, muy bien . . .

Teaching and learning modes

iii. After all the new vocabulary has been explained, preferably using context, but also with images, sounds, etc., go on to brainstorming new vocabulary to do with the theme.

Profe:	Vamos a ver si podemos reagrupar un máximo de palabras sobre este tema. ¿Quién puede proponerme palabras?
Jane:	Billete.
Profe:	Bien.
Théo:	¿Tarifa?
Profe:	Excelente
Mahmoud:	¿Como se dice "season ticket", Señora?
Profe:	¡Vamos! ¿Quién puede ayudar? … ¿Nadie? Claro, vamos a ponerlo aquí y después intentáremos buscarlo solo …

iv. Quiet working time while students find more words, and also look up new words or words they didn't know, using multimedia resources or dictionaries. Then, another quiet working time while they look for information. The information could be on the web (a webquest, see Chapter 10), or on paper, or in reference books. You will have prepared a hint sheet, giving them ideas of the information to find, and also sheets to record the new information.

Profe:	Voy a dividiros en pequeños grupos de trabajo. Cada grupo debe buscar las informaciones sobre los transportes en común en un ciudad española. Tenéis 10 (15/20) minutos para esta búsqueda de informaciones. El grupo A, es Debbie, Ava, Alison, Andy, y vais a tomar Sevilla, Grupo B, es Ben, Sophie … y hacéis búsqueda sobre Bilbao. Id a buscar la informaciones y llenad las grillas de información.

v. Then, a relatively quiet working time while they prepare a presentation of their information.

Profe:	Vale, muy bien. Ahora, necesitáis un miembro en cada grupo como portavoz. Los otros, vais a ayudarlo a prepararse. Tenéis 10 minutos.

vi. The plenary session makes them more open and actively engaging with the information.

> **Profe:** Ahora cada portavoz va a darnos detalles buscados por su grupo. Durante su presentación, vosotros otros, notáis los detalles. Luego, vamos a comparar la situación en las ciudades elegidas.

vii. And the session would end with a discussion about the information found. Which town was found to have the most variety in public transport? The most expensive? The worst? The most used? . . . You will have prepared prompts, if they are necessary. You could have the students as discussion-masters too.

> **Profe:** Discutimos de lo que hemos aprendido. ¿Hay algo que os habéis sorprendido?

These two lesson plans are adaptable to different situations – you might prefer to have several different succeeding patterns, especially if you have a class with a shorter attention span! Another alternative is to have blocks of group activity interspersed with plenary moments.

CHAPTER 4

Assessment

The learning process inevitably is subject to assessment of some kind. It is a cognitive act, whereas marking is a social act. That assessment can take many forms, and can lead to external certification, as in the International Baccalaureate, GCSE, or A-level, but leading up to this final assessment are many other forms, including the following.

- *Diagnostic assessment* – this is often used at the start of the learning process in order to find out where the individual students are and where they need to go. The result may influence lesson content, support needed, suggestions for remedial work, and course direction.

- *Self-assessment* – encouraging students to look at their own work can be very revealing. They are often very (too) critical. It is therefore advisable to give them positive ways of doing this. For example, a written task such as writing a letter could be done in draft form, then students can be given a sheet with common problems and asked to look at their draft in the light of these criteria before finalising their work.

- *Peer-assessment* – as above, peer-assessment needs to be carefully guided to make sure that it is based on criteria and not friendship or worse.

- *Portfolio development* – several types of portfolio exist and one of the most revealing about a student's ability is the "showcase" type, where a student places in his portfolio examples of work that he feels particularly happy with. (See below.)

- *Summative assessment* – usually takes place at the end of a teaching sequence, and often at the end of a larger period of work, such as end of term.

- *Formative assessment* – is usually seen as an ongoing process and occurs during the teaching sequence. A homework can be part of formative assessment.

The type of assessment involved leads to an effect on the learning process called washback. Washback can be negative or positive. For example, a summative assessment involving multiple-choice questions is likely to have the effect that some classroom activities will include this type of exercise. A performance-based test will have the washback effect of this kind of task taking place in the classroom. It is therefore all the more important to understand and to use the washback effect positively, by choosing assessment forms that reflect classroom practice and vice versa.

Most certificative assessments are summative in that they take place at the end of a learning process, however brief that process may be. It is often thought that certificative assessments are taken more seriously, because of their influence on the student's future. They are seen as high-stakes in a way that the other assessments are not. This is why it is all the more important to ensure that they are written correctly, developed to be feasible by all students, reliable in their results and valid in what they assess. We now take these last three qualities in order.

- *Validity* has many forms, but the overriding element is that the assessment "does what it says on the tin" – that it assesses what it says it will. The assessment will gain credibility if it does this, and the students will take it more seriously, answering the questions or performing the tasks more carefully than if they think it is a waste of time or unfair.

- *Reliability* concerns the decision taken on the basis of the assessment. Again, if a test is valid, the result of it is probably reliable. A further element in this is that the same teacher marks all the tests accurately, and that a group of teachers mark consistently with each other.

- Likewise for *feasibility* in its most obvious form: a test has to be "doable" by the students. However, it also has to be doable by the teacher and the institution, without too much time being taken up, or needing too much material, etc.

All of these terms are seen as continua and all assessments are the result of compromises made regarding them. Validity and reliability go together very well, but a really valid and reliable test, such as a live performance task, may not be feasible. Compromises always have to be made.

Let's focus more specifically on the two types of assessment that most teachers are likely to use in a classroom situation: summative and formative. An important difference between the two is whether they result in a "score"; by its nature, the former almost always does, whereas the latter may well not (see below). It is formative assessment that is of greatest interest to us here. However, to clear the ground, we'll first take a brief look at summative.

Summative assessment

The main purposes of summative assessment are:

- to assess students' knowledge and skills against defined criteria
- to identify individual and group strengths and weaknesses
- to monitor the success of various teaching methods
- to use as a planning tool for future work – this implies leaving spaces in teaching plans marked "Development" and "Remedial". This is particularly true when they take place at the end of a school term and the students will be back after a short break to continue their studies. In this way, they rejoin diagnostic assessment (see above).

The following general guidelines may be helpful.

- Always regard assessment as a normal part of teaching and learning, not as something added at intervals.
- Focus normally on one skill at a time and use the current activity to assess and record progress in it.
- Always be clear which elements of a skill you wish to assess – for the National Curriculum (NC) the criteria are provided by the Level Descriptions.
- Almost all the activities in this book exercise, and can be used to assess, more than one skill. Similarly, the four NC Attainment Targets (ATs) may be labelled "Listening", "Speaking", "Reading" and "Writing", but the Descriptions frequently call for several skills. Remember that a student's response may show her/him to be at quite different Levels in different skills.
- An example of a test that doesn't test what's intended: a listening test in which a lot of reading has to be done doesn't assess listening primarily. On the other hand, a reading test in which students have to DO something with what they have understood really does test comprehension. It also encourages students to really work on their comprehension if it is important for what follows.
- Above all, remember that "tests" that don't increase your insight into students' knowledge can hardly be worth doing. This is especially true of listening and reading comprehension tests.
- A checklist or grid is useful as a summary of Levels achieved by students, but it is not a good tool for recording their progress towards a given Level. For this, individual record sheets, with sections for each skill, are much more efficient. You can note what students can do or cannot yet do and so plan their future work more effectively. The sheets also form a cumulative record that can be passed on from one year to the next, perhaps as a part of your school's existing system. (See also "European Languages Portfolio" below.)

Assessing language skills

The various language skills call for different methods of assessment.

- In *listening* and *speaking/interacting*, you cannot hope to assess the levels of large numbers at the same time, and on–off individual oral tests are very time-consuming and not at all accurate. Aim for several tests over time to build a more accurate picture of true ability. It comes as no surprise that many assessment specialists call for a multiplicity of assessments, which in turn fits neatly with the Portfolio as developed below. Opting for a multiplicity of assessments doesn't mean assessing all the time. Rather, small-scale and low-stake assessment can occur incidentally and/or intentionally, at any time, allowing the student and the teacher to build up a clear picture of the former's true ability. For any activity involving discussion in pairs or groups, develop systems that allow you to home in unobtrusively on one group at a time.

- To assess *reading* a different approach is needed. Most course-books, and especially authentic materials taken from magazines or the Internet, provide plenty of interesting material from which specific reading skills can be assessed, for example the ability to identify details or to deduce meaning from context. From quite an early stage, however, students should be reading independently. For this your department needs to have a comprehensive reading scheme, with summary checklists and individual reading diaries in which students record and comment on what they have read. (See Chapter 15.)

- *Writing* appears the easiest skill to assess, in that you can check a whole class at the same time. However, it is important to set tasks that differentiate well across the range of ability of your students. Exercises with carefully prepared, closed answers are useful for introducing or reinforcing a structure, but they are quite unsuitable for assessment. Choose activities that move from guided to quite open-ended production, allowing each student to demonstrate what s/he is capable of.

Formative assessment

Formative assessment usually takes place during the learning process or after a short sequence. It is seen as more low-stakes than summative assessment and is likely to result in suggestions for remedial work or for stretching work, depending on how easy the student found it to do. It can take place at any time and might be based on classroom or on homework assignments. Formative assessment can include self- and peer-assessment. While these are not specifically required by the National Curriculum, they are implicit in many of the Programmes of Study,

especially Part 1/3(b–e), and students benefit enormously by being asked to evaluate their own work and that of others. As the Assessment for Learning (AfL)
Checklist[1] says:

> Assessment for learning is effective when pupils . . . are actively involved in formative
> assessment processes, eg setting targets, peer- or self-assessment, recognising progress
> in their written work, skills, knowledge and understanding.

The activities suggested in this book lend themselves to portfolio-based assessment. The European Languages Portfolio (ELP)[2] encourages students to reflect on
how they learn and gives examples of successfully completed activities. As the
ELP says, "an ELP is a personal document, in which students of all ages can record
their language learning and cultural experiences at school or outside school". This
is an extremely valuable experience for students, and it also provides you with an
ongoing record of how students see their own progress, which can be compared
to your assessments.

However, by their nature, individual portfolios are not conducive to
collaborative working, the main theme of this book. For this, peer-assessment is
much more productive, and it has one distinctive characteristic: where a
student is asked to assess another's work, the main formative benefit is that the
assessor benefits as much as, if not more than, the assessed. A few examples
follow.

- Any occasion when one student takes on the job of directing the activity of a
  group benefits all members, but particularly the "leader".

- An especially good example is in "serial dictation" (see Chapter 9, "Smaller
  groups"): the crucial stage is when student C corrects both A's pronunciation
  and B's text. This gives C training in listening and proof-reading, and of
  course A and B must concentrate too, because they may not agree with C's
  assessment.

- Some exercises lead to the production of a written report, with one student
  as "scribe", as in "re-creation of a text" or a project on a defined topic (see
  Chapter 9, "Larger groups"). Here it is the other members who must assess
  whether what the scribe is writing is both accurate factually and, even more,
  correct grammatically.

---

[1] www.webschool.org.uk/documents/aflchecklist.doc
[2] www.coe.int/t/dg4/education/elp and www.coe.int/t/dg4/portfolio/Default.asp?L=E&M=/main_
pages/welcome.html

The role of assessor is not easy for students, either socially or linguistically. Especially at first, it will be much more manageable if the assessment is limited to one or two points; for example, word order, the agreement of adjectives, the correct use of the cases of nouns or the past tenses of verbs. For the assessed student too, it is far better to concentrate on an element that has been the focus of the current activity or task. It is important not to put the students under stress to get everything right all the time.

CHAPTER 5

Use of the target language by students

The curriculum should provide opportunities for pupils to . . . communicate in the target language individually, in pairs, in groups and with speakers of the target language, including native speakers where possible, for a variety of purposes.[1]

The question of how much students (and the teacher) should use the target language has sometimes been a cause of controversy. It has been felt that concentrating on students' using the target language (which usually meant orally rather than in writing) would lead to neglect of grammatical structure, thus reducing the intellectual quality of the study of modern foreign languages. However, we believe that this is a false dichotomy – firm grasp of the "underlying model" can easily coexist with students' maximum use of the target language. Indeed, a good grasp of structure is a prerequisite for proper communication. Many of the activities in this book, especially those in Chapter 20, are based on this principle.

Types of classroom language

First of all, it's important to distinguish between the main uses of the target language (see boxed examples below).

A *Your instructions to students* – to be understood, perhaps demanding short answers.

B *Students addressing you* – requests for help (especially on process and meaning) and common classroom transactions (apologies/excuses, permissions, etc.).

C *Student-to-student language* – needed to communicate with each other in the target language, especially in group/pair/drama work (all the common functions, games-operating phrases, etc.). This is by some way the most

---

[1]   Modern Foreign Languages Programme of Study: key stage 3 (2008) §4b.

important type of students' language, as it directly affects their ability to learn and operate in the target language. It especially enhances their ability to develop "compensation strategies", enabling them to find ways of expressing themselves even when they don't know a particular word or phrase. These compensation strategies also increase the cognitive awareness of the student.

Par exemple ...   *LE LANGAGE DE LA SALLE DE CLASSE ...*

A Adam, lève-toi ! Sam, ferme la porte, s'il te plaît. Écoutez, tout le monde. Répondez en français, s'il vous plaît ! Formez vos groupes !

B Je m'excuse d'être en retard. Voulez-vous répéter, s'il vous plaît ? *Xxxxx*, c'est quoi en anglais/français ? Je regrette, j'ai oublié/perdu mon bic/mon cahier/mes devoirs/ ...

C Je pense à quoi ? Non, c'est pas ça ! J'ai oublié le nom de ce machin-là – tu sais comment il s'appelle ? C'est à moi/toi maintenant. À moi/toi de poser les questions ! As-tu du papier/un bic ? Donne-moi les cartes, s'il te plaît.

Zum Beispiel ...   *DIE SPRACHE DES KLASSENZIMMERS ...*

A Setz dich, Alfie! Josh, mach bitte das Fenster auf! Schaut an die Tafel, alle! Antwortet nicht auf englisch bitte! Jetzt arbeiten wir in Gruppen!

B Verzeihung, dass ich zu spät zu komme! Könnten Sie das wiederholen, bitte! Wie heisst *Xxxxx* auf englisch/deutsch? Tut mir leid, ich habe meinen Kuli/mein Heft/meine Hausaufgaben/ ... vergessen/verloren.

C Woran denke ich? Richtig – wie hast du das bloss erraten? Wie heisst das da, weisst du's? Du bist jetzt dran! Ich stelle jetzt die Fragen! Hast du einen Gummi/einen Bleistift? Gib mir die Karten bitte.

Por ejemplo ...   *EL LENGUAJE DE LA AULA ...*

A ¡Levantate, Alan! Jean, abre la ventana, pos favor. ¡Escuchad todos! ¡No respondas en inglés, Carl! ¡Haced grupos! ¡Tomad vuestros cuadernos! ¡Mirad la pizarra!

B Siento haber legado tarde. Repita la pregunta, pos favor. *Xxxxx*, ¿cómo se dice en español/inglés? He olvidado/perdido mi boli/mi cuaderno/mis deberes/...

C ¿En qué pienso? ¡Si, tienes razon! ¿Cómo lo has adivinado? He olvidado cómo se llama este chismo – ¿lo sabes? ¿A quién le toca ahora? Me toca a mi/Te toca a ti. ¡Yo haré/Tú harás las preguntas! ¿Tienes papel/un boli/una goma de borrar? ¡Dame las cartas, por favor!

Collecting and learning classroom language

Treat classroom language as a topic in its own right, one that pervades every other topic and must be constantly revised and added to. Remember that students cannot use the appropriate language if they have not learnt it. An effective way of keeping classroom language in students' minds is to display sections of it on posters around the room. These displays are best prepared by students, who should devote discrete sections of their vocabulary books to this core language, to be learnt and used. (See also Chapter 19.)

Core language

These "chunks" of high-frequency language recur time and time again in every sort of context. Students need to record and learn them systematically, and to use them consciously in their work, especially in writing. Apart from the classroom language listed above, a few other examples:

- *One can/cannot/must/must not ...*
- *In my opinion ... /I think that ... because ...*
- *There is/are (not) ...*
- *... more/less ... than .../as ... as ...*
- Impersonal verbs
- Prepositions of place, time, relationships ...
- Common conjunctions, especially *when, before, while, after*
- *If* + Present > Future, progressing later to Past > Conditional (Perfect).

Helping students to persevere with the target language

- Use English for specific purposes, and make clear *why* it is used. Agree with students a clear signal that indicates when English is allowed – for example, a reversible card hung on the board (Union flag/flag of the other country, *EN/TL*, etc.).
- Present classroom language in manageable chunks related to specific activities, to be (re-)learnt as part of students' preparation for carrying them out.
- List any terms or phrases that are essential for a particular topic, and have students copy them into their vocabulary notebooks and perhaps create displays listing them. Students could suggest in English the phrases they need, and you supply the target language.
- Agree procedures that favour the target language and discourage English. Start with interchanges between you and the students (A and B above).

When the *TL* sign is up, you "can't understand" when spoken to in English, and if the student is really stumped, and the phrase could be useful, take the opportunity to add it to the class's core language.

- Provide ample opportunities for students to feed back or to give opinions on topics using key opinion phrases taught. Students often like to give their thoughts! This is best done in groups and set as a competitive activity to extend the conversation, through each student having to ask whether the other(s) agree or disagree, giving reasons why.

This last suggestion is in line with the "Group Talk" approach developed by Greg Horton at Wildern School, Hants. Students work in small groups, this being facilitated by an appropriate classroom layout. A stimulus (a theme, or a film, or an image, or a controversial topic) is given and pupils react spontaneously and openly about that subject. This gives rise to more genuine language use as they are prompted, if not provoked, to agree/disagree, justify, argue their case, debate, etc. The target language alone is accepted, the learners debate and conjecture freely, interaction being the name of the game. There is no set finishing time: the teacher manages the whole thing and calls time when the interaction seems to be petering out. Support is given by key phrases being put on the walls of the classroom, within the eye-lines of the pupils. Care needs to be taken that the weaker students are not "outvoiced" by the stronger ones, but this kind of classroom event promotes real-world use of language within the range of the learner's developmental interest.

A common objection to students' using the target language in group work has been that "it just reinforces error". But in a practical subject errors are not just inevitable, they are useful to the teacher, who monitors written *and* oral work and notes recurrent errors to be remedied. Even more importantly, students need to be encouraged to recognise that making mistakes is part of and even essential to the learning process, and to learn how to profit by them.

CHAPTER 6

Training the ear, training the voice

Pupils should be able to ... use correct pronunciation and intonation.[1]

Much of the point (and pleasure) of using a foreign language is lost if the speaker's accent is poor. Younger students especially are adept at distinguishing and producing the sounds of a foreign language, but they need systematic training, from the start, before adolescent embarrassment sets in. Build up their confidence progressively and repeatedly.

Hearing the difference

Recognising new sounds in a foreign language is the first step towards being able to pronounce them. Concentrate on sounds and sound-combinations that do not occur in students' L1 – for example, French *u/ou*, nasal vowels, dental *t/d* and unaspirated *t/p*; German *ö/ü/u*, *ich-/ach-* sounds and glottal stop; Spanish *s/z*, *h/j*, *b/β* and *d/p*; Russian ы, hard л and sibilants. A few hints follow.

- Write up and number the sounds to be practised – two or at most three – then pronounce suitable words (including invented ones) and ask various students to say the number of the sound they heard. This will give you a first idea of their aural discrimination.

- Use *known* words, especially "transparent words" (cognates), to practise a given sound, then unfamiliar or even invented words to test (as in the boxed example below).

- To assess this more precisely, get students to set up (quickly!) a score-chart like that shown below – here with 10 words containing two contrasting sounds, but adaptable to any configuration. Students enter a circle for their own answer, then a cross (+) for the correct answer given at the end. The number of "hot cross buns" is their score. The completed charts give a very

---

[1]   Modern Foreign Languages Programme of Study: key stage 3 (2008) §2.2d.

clear indication of each student's level of aural discrimination, as well as of the sounds needing further work.

SCORE-CHART

	1	2	3	4	5	6	7	8	9	10
A										
B										

Par exemple ... 　　　　　　*UN PETIT QUIZ ACOUSTIQUE ...*

Maintenant, j'ai un petit quiz pour vous. Pour commencer, recopiez dans vos cahiers la table que j'ai mise sur le tableau blanc. Mettez «OU» dans une ligne et «U» dans l'autre. Mais faites vite ! ... OK, maintenant vous allez entendre dix mots – est-ce ils contiennent «ou» ou «u» ? Mettez un petit cercle dans la case pour «ou» ou dans la case pour «u». Prêts ? Numéro 1 «vous» ... 2 «tout» ... 3 «tu» ... 4 «vu» ... 5 «poussin» ... 6 «prunelle» ... 7 «vupot» ... 8 «troutogars» ... 9 «moupsie» ... 10 «bubaie». . . . . . . Maintenant, j'écris les réponses correctes sur la tableau blanc, et vous mettez une petite croix dans la case qu'il faut. Numéro 1: OU . . . . . .

Producing the sounds

- "Creep up" on *individual sounds*, aiming for increasing accuracy. Most new sounds are best approached from "neighbouring" sounds in English (or another L1). For example:
  - [spread lips] EN *ee* → [round lips] FR *u*/GM long *ü* → *ee* → *u/ü* . . . . . .
  - [tongue back] EN *oo* → [tongue forward] FR *u*/GM long *ü* → *oo* → *u/ü*
  - [exaggerated forward *h*] EN *Hee* → [intermediate stage] *iHee* → GM *ich*
  - [exaggerated back *h*] EN *Haa* → [intermediate stage] *aHaa* → GM *ach*
  - [retroflex tongue] EN *apple* → [hybrid word] *appoolampa* → RU лампа

- The unaspirated *t* and *p* of French and other languages often make difficulties. Get students to hold their open hand close to their mouth and say, for example, English *petty* and feel the puff of air produced; then say French *petit*, trying to reduce the puff as much as possible. Such exercises give students positive feedback on their performance.

- Embed contrasting sounds in *words*. Use familiar "transparent words" (cognates) – or even invent some. Get students to say one of two or three words, others to identify which and repeat it – in groups? You say a word, students say whether it is in a previously studied sentence or not (see boxed example below).

Training the ear and voice

- Embed the same words in *phrases,* if possible from the current topic. Prepositional/adverbial phrases are especially suitable. Practise phrase intonation – in some languages phrases sound like long words.

- The key to *sentence* production is correct intonation. Get students to catch the sentence rhythm – perhaps contrasted with a similar English sentence. At later stages, have a native speaker record students' written work, as a model for them.

- The use of song with younger language learners in particular is ideal for learning pronunciation patterns and intonation. The rhythm of a song can help to focus attention on pronunciation, intonation and fluency. Karaoke videos on YouTube and other video sites can be fun. The focus is on producing accurate pronunciation rather than developing comprehension, thus allowing students to be able to tackle the pronunciation of new words independently.

Par exemple . . .   *ÉCOUTEZ BIEN. QU'EST-CE QUE VOUS ENTENDEZ? . . .*

Prof: Regardez cette phrase sur le tableau blanc – je vais la lire:

La voiture roulait lentement le long des rues désertes.

Maintenant, écoutez bien. Je vais prononcer quelques mots – s'ils sont dans la phrase, marquez une coche dans vos cahiers; si non, marquez une croix. Prêts ? OK !

roule . . . désert . . . long . . . roues . . . lentement . . .

rues . . . voiture . . . désertes . . . vautour . . . longue

Vous avez combien de coches ? 1 ? 2 ? 3 ? 4 ? 5 ? . . . Alors, il y avait 5 mots correctes, c'étaient *long, rues, lentement, voiture, désertes.* Tu as une question, Jo ?

Jo: Oui. J'ai entendu 'voiture' deux fois.

Prof: Ce que tu as entendu la deuxième fois, c'était 'vautour' – c'est une espèce d'oiseau! Cherche-le dans ton dico ou sur Google. Oui, Tom ?

Tom: J'ai 'rues' deux fois.

Prof: Mais non, Tom ! La première fois, c'était 'roues' – *ou / u // ou / u* – tu te rappelles ?

But *always . . .*

MAKE IT SHORT, SHARP AND FREQUENT – LONG-DRAWN PHONETICS CAN GET VERY BORING

Using recordings, including authentic items from the Internet (see also Chapter 13), distinguish between:

A aural discrimination

B listening for general meaning (possibly from a given list of topics) and type (instructions, incident, argument, description of persons/objects/scenery . . .) = "skimming"

C listening for specific information, as in most listening comprehension tests = "scanning"

D listening for specific elements of language = "parsing". (See also Chapter 20.)

These are not separate; you can easily start with one and then link in to another. For example, the rather dry-sounding "parsing" can well lead to discussion of the general "tone" of the passage ("skimming"), then home in on specific details ("scanning").

A prime benefit of using authentic recordings is in encouraging students to recognise the sound associated with a particular spelling, or the spelling associated with a particular sound. Students are used to learning in this way from primary level upwards and this "comfortable" aspect of the activity can be played on for language-learning. For this reason, dictation has its place in the language classroom; new ways of integrating it have been explored extensively, for example by Davis and Rinvolucri (1988, see "Further Reading"). Flashcards can make use of this technique, introducing the sound simultaneously with the written form. Try an individual activity using a recording and a script to identify, to take an easy example, the different spellings of the /z/ phoneme.

Training the ear and the voice can take some time, and it can be disconcerting for the individual student if done "in front of the class" rather than in a group. However, individual work can be promoted through a Virtual Learning Environment (see Chapter 10) and through encouraging the student to do some private work on these skills. The important thing is to make them an integral part of the learning process rather than leaving it to chance.

CHAPTER 7

Working together: General principles

This short chapter draws together ideas that are discussed more fully elsewhere in the book, hence the number of cross-references. It thus sets the scene for many of the other activities in this book.

Size and composition of groups

- *Pair-work* is a low-risk activity in that no-one else can really hear if you are making a mistake, lost for words, etc. It can therefore help students gain confidence. Pairs do not have to be fixed. Depending on the task concerned, an established pair can be separated.

- With pre-set question and answer, pair-work is useful for simple *practice* of learnt language. Make this work brisk, for example by allowing a very brief time and challenging students to complete as many exchanges as possible. However, pair-work can also produce more spontaneous *use* of language (see Chapter 8).

- *Groups of three or four* work well for more open-ended activities (see Chapter 9), increasing to perhaps five or six for drama (see Chapter 12).

- The ideal *composition* of pairs and groups will depend on the activity. In some topics, practice of conversation strategies may be hindered if the members already know each other very well. In groups of three or more the students are less likely to be of equal ability; pairs, on the other hand, can be deliberately composed of students of equal or mixed ability, according to the demands of the task.

- In *small-group work*, students take it in turn to be evaluator and helper to the others, acting as surrogate teacher, controlling questions and answers, supplying information, awarding or deducting points, checking for use of English, keeping scores, etc. This "lead student" may use a set of possible answers to a role-play to help and assess the others. A student can also be the group reporter, reporting back to whole-class sessions, for example.

However, students need careful training if they are to carry out any of these roles successfully (see next section).

Setting up and monitoring

- Even with well-practised classes, it is important to set up pair- and group-work carefully and to monitor it at all stages. (See boxed example below.)

- Explain the activity clearly, especially the role of "group leader" – sometimes one group can be used to demonstrate what to do. The OHP or interactive whiteboard can also be very useful here.

- Give each student a letter within the group: A/B/C/ ... This makes it much easier to define each role, control the starting order and the change of role, and bring the activity to an end.

- It is almost always good to start with a brief period of individual *"rumination time"* – that can be as short as 30 seconds – to allow students to think about what they are going to do and say. For more demanding tasks, this preparation time can be part of homework.

- Allow the groups to get going on their own, but ensure that all are working.

- Move from group to group, helping, correcting, encouraging and assessing as you go.

- Evaluate and record where it went well and where not so well, and why.

Par exemple ...   *FORMEZ VOS GROUPES ! ...*

Écoutez tout le monde ! Vous allez travailler en groupes de 3. Vous savez tous quelle lettre vous avez ? Toi, Jessica, tu as A, B ou C ? B ? Bien, cette fois, c'est B qui commence. Tous les B, vous pensez à quelque chose par rapport au camping – c'est notre thème d'aujourd'hui, n'est-ce pas ? Vous pensez à cette chose, *mais vous ne dites pas ce que c'est* – c'est à A et C de vous poser des questions pour le découvrir. Compris, tout le monde ? Bien, je vous donne 30 secondes, les B pour choisir un objet ou une action, les A et les C pour penser aux questions que vous allez poser. ...
... OK, allez-y ! Les A, posez votre première question. ...... OK, finissez ! Maintenant les C pensent à quelque chose, et les A et les B posent les questions. ......

For some students their first experience of pair- and especially group-work can be quite intimidating, the more so if they are not familiar with the vocabulary and structures needed for the activity. So be sure to teach them the necessary language before they plunge in – as a French lecturer once told his audience: "On ne leur demande pas d'inventer le français !"

CHAPTER 8

Semi-spontaneous pair-work

Pair-work needs to be meaningful in order to succeed, and if the two members of the pair have slightly different tasks, which complement each other, this can avoid some of the dangers of unequal completion of the task. The work can range from very tightly controlled to much more open-ended. Equally, pairs can remain together for the whole exercise ("Fixed partners"), or partners may change during the course of it ("Multiple partners"). This chapter offers ideas across the whole range.

Fixed partners

Pre-set dialogues

This is the most basic level: pairs work with pre-set questions and answers, which usually mirror a structure or lexis that you have just been introducing or revising with the class. Student A thus takes over the role of teacher, with B as the student. These dialogues need to be short and sharp – set a brief time limit and ask how many repetitions each pair can do. This prevents the exercise from becoming too boring, and is an effective way of embedding a new structure. It also gives good practice in question and answer intonation.

Par exemple . . .   *DIALOGUES PRÉSCRITES . . .*

[Se répètent pendant 10/20/. . . secondes.]

Passé composé avec être

A: Qu'est-ce que tu as fait hier ?   B: *Je suis allé(e)* en ville. . . . . . .

Modal 'POUVOIR' + Infinitif

A: Tu viens au disco ce soir ?   B: Non, je ne *peux* pas *danser*, j'ai une entorse

à la cheville . . . . . .

Zum Beispiel ...   *FESTE DIALOGE ...*

[Wiederholen sich 10/20/ ... Sekunden lang.]

Perfekt mit <u>sein</u>

A: Was hast du gestern gemacht?   B: Ich <u>bin</u> in die Stadt <u>gegangen</u>.......

<u>weil</u> mit Verb in Endstellung

A: Warum bist du nicht in die   B: <u>Weil</u> ich kein Geld <u>habe</u>!
Disko gekommen?

Por ejemplo ...   *DIÁLOGOS PRESCRITOS*

[Se repiten durante 10/20/ ... segundos.]

Dos objetos de la tercera persona

A: ¿Has enviado el dinero a Miguel?   B: Sí, <u>se lo</u> envié ayer.......

Objeto directo personal con <u>a</u>

A: ¿Conoces <u>a</u> mi amigo Javier?   B: No, pero encontré ayer <u>a</u> su hermana.

Responses within a defined situation

This gives students a chance to use what they have learnt more spontaneously. Role A can be prescribed by you while role B is more open, or only the situation is set and A invents the stimulus. Both roles can easily be related to the current topic or structure, and both can be given as much support as you judge necessary. In many of these activities, students will benefit from having a brief "ruminating" time in which to prepare.

- A has been hurt or is ill, B is the doctor asking questions, perhaps prescribing a remedy. [WHERE? WHEN? HOW LONG? YOU MUST ...] (See boxed example below.)

- A has lost something or it has been stolen, B takes down details, gives advice. [WHERE? WHEN? DESCRIPTIONS OF PEOPLE AND/OR ARTICLES.]

- A makes a statement (like/dislike, opinion), B must disagree, give reasons, ask questions. [... WHY? ... BECAUSE ...]

- A has a problem, B gives advice. [YOU MUST / OUGHT TO ... I CAN'T ...] (For a similar, written exercise, see "To-and-fro dialogues" in Chapter 9, LARGER GROUPS.)

- Prepare two versions of a passage, in each of which portions of text alternate with blanks. Version A's blanks correspond to version B's text, and vice versa. Students sit back-to-back in pairs, A dictates her/his first portion and B writes it into her/his first blank; then B dictates and A writes, and so on. At the end, A and B compare and correct their versions. [PRACTISING PRONUNCIATION, LINKING SOUND TO SCRIPT.] (For an example of this exercise, see box in Chapter 3, X-SHAPED LESSON.)

- A and B each receive, face down, a set of three picture-cards showing various activities. Each also writes down three clock times – in the morning, afternoon/evening, middle of the night. A, using her/his list, asks *"What were you doing at . . . ?"*, B turns over her/his *first* card and describes the activity, which s/he then has to justify in the face of A's disbelief. [WHAT WERE YOU DOING AT . . .? (PRACTICE OF IMPERFECT) AT *that* HOUR? WHY? WHO WERE YOU WITH? . . .] See boxed example below – pic-cards are given for just one student, timings for the other. Conversations will go better if students are given time to prepare, perhaps for homework. The school's art department may well be able to help by producing suitable pic-cards in multiple copies.

- A and B have a map, and A is asking B how to get from X to Y. B is given (or invents) information about times and prices, as well as about various problems (delays, accidents, traffic restrictions, weather, etc.). B makes suggestions, A responds appropriately. [WHEN? FROM/TO WHERE? HOW MUCH? HOW LONG? WHY NOT? . . .]

- Many similar "incomplete information" activities can be devised to fit the current topic, so as to produce more spontaneous speech.

Par exemple . . .   *CHEZ LE MÉDECIN . . .*

Médecin: Bonjour, mademoiselle, qu'est-ce qui vous amène aujourd'hui ?/Que puis-je faire pour vous ?/Qu'est-ce qui s'est passé ? . . .

Malade: J'ai mal à la jambe.

Médecin: Où exactement ?/Faites voir/Montrez-moi . . .

Malade: Ici, à la cheville.

Médecin: Vous faisiez quoi? Vous êtes tombée? . . .

Malade: Je jouais au tennis avec mon ami/Je faisais du vélo/. . . et je suis tombée/ . . .

Médecin: Cela fait mal si j'appuie ici ?

Malade: Aïe !!

Médecin: D'accord. C'est pas cassé – peut-être fêlé./Je vais vous faire passer une radio pour être certain./C'est tout simplement une petite entorse./Vous devez vous reposer pendant cinq jours, ne pas jouer, ne pas marcher.

Par exemple?...   *QU'EST-CE QUE TU FAISAIS À …?*

Figure 8.1 Fishing

Figure 8.2 Books

Figure 8.3 Football

Élève B: Alors, dis-moi, qu'est-ce que tu faisais à 7 heures et demie ce matin ?

Élève A: J'allais à la pêche.

   B: Quoi ? Si tôt ? Tu ne pouvais pas le faire à une heure plus raisonnable ?

   A: Non non! C'est à cette heure que les poissons viennent à la surface! On voit bien que tu n'es pas pêcheur !......

   B: Et à 15h45, qu'est-ce que tu faisais ?

   A: Je viens d'écrire un livre, et cet après-midi j'ai reçu les premiers exemplaires.

   B: Tu es écrivain ! Quel est le sujet de ton livre ?

   A: C'est l'histoire des vies privées et secrètes de tous mes copains.

   B: Quoi !! Tu veux dire, tu as raconté tout ce je t'ai dit de mes vacances à Paris ?!

   A: Mais bien sûr! Mes lecteurs adorent le scandale ! ......

   B: Et à 11h55, tu faisais quoi ?

A: Je jouais au football.

B: Au milieu de la nuit! Tu veux rire !

A: Non, c'est vrai. Demain c'est le championnat régional – et nous ne voulons pas arriver en dernier ! ......

Multiple partners

More open-ended activities

Changing partners during an activity gives great scope for students to use their initiative and show that they can adapt the language they've learnt in order to cope with unforeseen situations.

- An interesting "chain reaction" technique, applicable to many pair role-plays, goes like this:

  i. A_1 and B_1, A_2 and B_2, etc. work out possible roles on the set topic, making notes to support performance but not actually performing it.

  ii. All the As then move to the next pair in a clockwise direction and act out the role-play with their new partner. Clearly, although all students have prepared their own parts, none of them knows quite how the new partner will react, so they must be prepared to adapt accordingly.

  iii. This continues for a set number of moves, after which students evaluate how it went, what language they needed, etc. The number of moves can be regulated by grouping, say, three or four pairs together.

- Another widely applicable technique is "double pairs". For example:

  i.   "*Pros and cons*", "Pessimist vs Optimist". A and B prepare one viewpoint, with reasons (e.g., likes and dislikes), C and D the opposite, then come together to argue.

  ii. "*Moving house*". All pairs are issued with road-maps showing start X and destination Y, distances between mid-points, maximum road speeds, traffic conditions, height and weight restrictions, roadworks, etc. Each pair plans how to get a removal van of given height, width and loaded weight from X to Y in the shortest time. Pairs then compare their results and agree a best solution. (This is in itself a perfect example of a scenario and therefore of task-based language teaching – see next chapter.)

  iii. Among other possibilities: "*A meal for 8 people*" (guests' dietary requirements given, perhaps also a menu); "*Equipment for two couples*

> *camping for two weeks"* (budget, terrain, availability of shops, etc. could
> be specified); *"Planning a party"* (could be own age, children or old
> people); *"Eight rules for the classroom";* . . .

Pair-work has become a staple of language classrooms, but we have moved on from very closely guided role-plays to pair-work that involves real communication, exchanging information, and decision-making depending on the information received. In pair-work, as in group-work, the student really is a "social agent", in the words of the CEF. Most of the activities mentioned above involve a given set of circumstances, the parameters of the task. These circumstances are situated within a specific environment and are, in many cases, clearly linked to the real-world use of language that may confront the student.

CHAPTER 9

Some possibilities for group-work

How big is a group? Are there limits to group size? The answers will depend on the parameters of the task concerned. For example, if the task is to choose a new member of a band/social group/flat-share, etc., then the group working on the task will need to be larger and probably not a friendship group, whereas more personal tasks may be better tackled within a smaller, more intimate, friendship group. Before deciding on group size, parameters need to be identified, such as the need for trust, need for opposing ideas or ability to work as a team. An upper limit is normally six/seven people per group – it is harder for all members to make themselves heard if the group becomes too large.

Smaller groups (three/four)

It can be quite surprising to see what a difference adding just one member to a pair makes to the possible activities. The third member ("C") can act as monitor/ peer assessor, for example allotting plus/minus points for use of the target language/English. S/he also allows the other two to compete in all sorts of ways, adding a certain spice to exercises that otherwise might be less interesting.

All the following suggestions can easily be linked with the current topic. Many can produce *a joint written account* – one member can act as scribe, but all are responsible for the text.

- *Guesswork*: Student C thinks of a person, object, etc. A and B put *"Yes/No"* questions or other questions until one guesses correctly.

- *What's in my mind?* C puts open-ended questions, makes *True/False* statements, describes some person or object, etc., from the current topic or general knowledge; A and B race to answer.

- *Serial dictation*: Prepare a series of sentences labelled $A1/2/3/\ldots$, $B1/2/3/\ldots$, $C1/2/3/\ldots$, as many as required, each series on separate sheets. (More able/ older students can compose their own sentences.) A now dictates her/his first one (A1) to B, who writes it down. Without reference to A's text, C then corrects both A's pronunciation and B's text as s/he thinks fit (*training in listening and proof-reading*). Then B dictates B1 to C (same procedure), C dictates C1 to A, etc., etc. The results can be taken in for assessment or checked by the students against the originals.

- *Picture study*: All have a short time to study a picture, which is then withdrawn. Each individual group member then writes down answers to set questions (easier) or writes notes on the main facts (harder). They then compare what they have written and try to reach agreement, before checking from the picture. (See photo and box in Chapter 14.)

- *Creating a sketch*: Group agrees roles for a sketch, each member prepares own role (if possible set for homework), group works out sketch and performs it using only brief prompts or symbols (*not* full scripts).

- *Personal narratives*: All members prepare notes (if possible for homework) about personal details, likes and dislikes (preferably with reasons), a past experience, future plans, thoughts/words suggested by a picture or sound recording, etc. Each in turn then presents to the group, again using only prompts. Others make notes to help recall of the presentation, at levels ranging from single words and phrases heard up to summaries of the main points of the talk.

- *Consequences*: The traditional headings for this game are *"X met Y at ...",* *"She said to him ...", "He said to her ...", "The consequence was ...",* but these can be varied, as can the numbers in a group. Each member writes a line for the first heading, then folds the paper over so as to conceal what s/he has written and passes it on to the next member, who does the same for the next heading, and so on for the other headings. At the end the papers are unfolded and the results read out. (Be ready for some possibly "rude" entries!)

- *Re-creation of a text*: A sequence of activities combining reading, speaking, writing and vocabulary learning:
  i. reading of original text (in class or for homework)
  ii. whole-class exploration by question and answer, with full use of text, notes made, reference works, etc. Looking up, noting and later learning of vocabulary
  iii. [*essential stage*] oral re-creation in groups, with *diminishing* use of text, repeated until the group is satisfied
  iv. written re-narration, jointly by group (with one member as scribe), then individually, *without* reference to original
  v. re-correction from original, assessed re-narration, ...
  vi. further development if appropriate: comparison with related texts, continuation as free composition ...

- *Language Charades*: described by Peggy Buckwalter[1] as a university activity, adapted here to make it more suitable for use in schools. (See boxed example below.)

  i. Each student in the group is given a slip of paper describing a different problematic situation in note form. This can easily be related to the current topic.

  ii. They take it in turns to be the "speaker", who describes this situation to the others, using only the target language. To make it easier, mime may be allowed. The "listeners" do not interrupt at this stage, they just listen carefully.

  iii. When the speaker has finished, the listeners ask questions, also in the target language, to check on their understanding.

  iv. When the listeners feel they have understood the situation described by the speaker, they summarise it, either in the target language or in English.

  v. Another member of the group then becomes speaker.

For example . . .   *LANGUAGE CHARADES: ON HOLIDAY . . .*

En français

En vacances avec parents. Se promener dans la ville – seul(e). Perdre son chemin. Oublier le nom de l'hôtel. Entrer dans un magasin. Décrire l'hôtel. Téléphoner à l'hôtel. Appeler un taxi. Rentrer à l'hôtel.

Auf deutsch

Ferien am Meer. Baden gehen. Strömung sehr stark. Nicht an Strand wieder gelangen können. Schreien – keiner hört. Eine kleine Insel sehen. Auf die Felsen steigen – kalt. Endlich ein Schiff. Ein warmes Getränk geben. Zum Hafen zurückbringen.

En español

De vacaciones en Madrid. Pequeño hotel. Salir para comprar un periódico. Dejar pasaporte en el cuarto. Volver al hotel. Pasaporte desaparecido. Llamar a la policía. Interrogar a todo el personal. Buscar por todas partes. Pasaporte debajo de la cama.

Larger groups (five/six/seven)

Groups of this size can be treated as small classes and can undertake activities beyond the scope of smaller groups. On the other hand, they can carry out activities that would be quite tedious or unworkable in a whole class.

---

[1] Peggy Buckwalter, in *Vida Hispánica*, ALL, Autumn 2007, p. 9.

Possibilities for group-work

- *Surveys*: Members carry out a survey within the group and record results (see also Chapter 11, "Class surveys").

- *Chain sentences*: Each member repeats the existing sentence and adds an item. The final sentence can then be written out.

- *To-and-fro dialogues*: Roles X and Y are defined beforehand (e.g., X = parent waiting up, Y = teenager arriving home very late). Sitting in a ring, each member writes a first line for role X on a sheet of paper and passes it to the left. Each then writes a suitable reply for role Y and passes it back to the right. This is repeated for a given time or number of lines, when the dialogues can be performed. (See boxed example below. For the sake of simplicity, this assumes a ring of only three, of which only two exchanges are shown, but the size can range from this to the whole class – the only essential is that the two ends of the chain are linked.)

- *Chain/cumulative narration*: Both the preceding two techniques can be used to reconstruct a previously studied oral or written text or (re-)tell a known story (see Chapter 16). The stories can be "seeded" by giving the first line; support can be given by providing skeleton prompts.

- *Language games using cards*: Pelmanism*, Happy Families, Snap, etc. It is important that all games should provide "linguistic gain", for example by demanding that players say what the card represents in order to retain it or gain the point. (*See Chapter 19, "Use of definitions".)

- *Defined projects*, usually based on the current topic. Each member of the group has a role suited to her/his capabilities – coordination, research, graphics (including publicity), materials . . . Examples of topics: setting up and stocking stalls in a market; planning a new village or town district; planning a youth mag/school newspaper; planning an expedition/adventure holiday; planning a publicity campaign for a new product or for your town/area.

For example . . . TO-AND-FRO DIALOGUES between A, B AND C . . .

[← C (= Y)] B (= X) → ← A (= Y) C (= X) → ← B (= Y) [A (= X) →]

Papel X: *Mi novio me engaña.*	Rolle X: *Meine Freundin betrügt mich.*
Papel Y: Amiga-Confidente.	Rolle Y: Freund-Vertrauter.
X: ¡Estoy tan desgraciada!	X: Ich glaub', ich habe ein Problem.
Y: ¿Por qué? ¿Tus padres te dan lata?	Y: Was für ein Problem? Du bist knapp bei Kasse?
X: No, peor.	X: Diesmal nicht. Viel schlimmer.
Y: ¿Pues qué? ¿Te falta un vestido para la tarde?	Y: Mach doch kein so grosses Geheimnis daraus! Was ist's, dieses Problem?

X: ¡No, no! ¡No seas tonta! Es mi novio.

Y: ¿Y ...? Está enfermo?

X: Es que ... le vi con una chica.

Y: ¿Y qué? Debe de conocer multitudes de chicas.

X: Pero, ¡la besaba!

Y: Era quizás su hermana.

X: ¡Una hermana no se besa así!

Y: A propósito, ¡como se llama, tu novio?

X: Juan García.

Y: ¡¡A!! Yo ... no sabía que ...

X: ¡Dios mío! ¡Eras tú – traidora!

X: Meine Freundin betrügt mich, ich bin absolut sicher.

Y: Sie hat Schluss gemacht?

X: Nicht gerade – aber sie hat einen Brief gekriegt.

Y: Und du kriegst nie Briefe!

X: Ja doch, aber sie ist rot geworden, und sie wollte ihn mir nicht zeigen.

Y: Sag mal, dieser Brief, war er handgeschrieben oder getippt?

X: Getippt, glaub'ich.

Y: Ein getippter Liebesbrief! Das wäre was Neues!

X: Aber warum wollte sie mir den Brief nicht zeigen?

Y: Ich auch, ich habe einen getippten Brief gekriegt – gestern. Ich habe falsch geparkt und muss 20 Euro zahlen. Ich wette, sie hat dasselbe gemacht, und sie wollte es dir nicht sagen.

Scenarios

The *scenario* is another form of group-work that can also be used in an individual fashion. In a scenario, the students:

- look for information
- work with that information (selecting what is relevant, rejecting the rest)
- exchange the information with the other members of the group
- discuss the information and the possible solution to the problem
- reveal the proposed solution in a plenary oral session and/or in a written form.

Many different forms of scenario exist, but as a group activity, one of the most successful forms is as follows.

i. A theme is chosen, probably from the current topic, and a realistic situation identified within the theme. This situation is usually a problem that needs to be solved. "Problem" is used here in the broadest sense – it might be the creation of a tourist brochure, for example.

ii. Roles for the mission are proposed. This can be very useful, particularly with adolescents, as students take on new identities with their roles and therefore can suggest ideas that are not their own. This means they can take more risks than they usually would. If the scenario is a group one, several roles and names are developed.

iii. A set of essential documents or resources is made available to the group. These can be audio, video, text. You can also take on the role of resource-provider, students having to ask questions to get essential information.

iv. Each student in the group takes on the task of getting information from one source. The members of the group exchange the information they have found, leading to lots of interaction and use of communication strategies. They discuss it, disagreeing, justifying, reformulating, summarising as they go.

v. They elect a spokesperson to communicate their decision to the whole class, helping her/him to prepare for this monologue and supporting her/him as s/he describes their ideas, providing back-up when necessary.

vi. The whole group prepares a written report of the proposed solution.

For example ...   *AN ADVENTURE HOLIDAY ...*

Mission: You and your colleagues are on work experience in a company specialising in mini-break adventure holidays for children. The company wants to add a new event to its list and has received two propositions, written in (French/German/Spanish/ ...). The company has asked you to investigate the two propositions and decide which is more likely to attract the clients. You need to get the information about this, discuss it, and reach a decision on which you all agree. An assessment sheet used by the company for all propositions is included for your use.

Phase 1: Using the dossier of information provided, make notes to get the information suggested on your assessment sheet. Each member of the group takes one aspect of the propositions.

Phase 2: Exchange the information that you have found. Make sure that everyone in the group understands the information exchanged. Ask for clarification if necessary.

Phase 3: Discuss which proposition is the best, in your view.

Phase 4: Present the results of your discussion to the whole class. Be prepared to justify your choice and to answer questions from the audience.

Phase 5: Write a mini-report to the company board of directors, giving details of your decision, including justifications.

The *dossier of information* provides:

- two very different adventure activity holidays for young people

- details of transport possibilities, etc.

- an assessment sheet in the form of information needed, but without direct questions.

Remember: In a scenario, there is no right or wrong answer. Any solution to the problem is acceptable, provided it is justified through use of the resource material. This gives students a sense of control over what they are doing with the language: you don't know what their interpretation of the task and the resource material will be; their result is truly unknown to everybody in the room but themselves. The language becomes not only a system to be learnt but also a real tool for communication and action.

Using ICT in the languages classroom

In this chapter we discuss many different ways of using ICT in the languages classroom, starting with the hardware and software. The next sections look at ideas for using them, finishing with a look at Virtual Learning Environments (VLEs).

Note: the whole world of ICT changes so fast that nothing we write here can be guaranteed to last for ever. We are sure, though, that you, with the help of your students, will be able to keep up-to-date and that the suggestions we make here will not date too much.

Hardware

Language laboratories

Even with an older language lab, you can incorporate exercises and activities as pre-tasks for a much wider task (see scenario work below). Modern laboratories are computerised and can enable pair-work to be more realistic (paired students can sit far apart, for example), or jigsaw listening, where students have different parts of a text, and so become experts in their own part. A follow-up activity is therefore to compare the information they have, or to exchange the information in order to put the jigsaw back together. Many labs have Internet access, enabling webquests to be carried out (see below). Most will record interactions for later assessment. No longer does every student have to listen to the same document: differentiation is made much easier in the choice of documents. Essentially, language labs continue to offer ease of individualisation, but they have become much more dynamic.

Carousel working

In Chapter 2, we mentioned that ICT can take its place in a carousel. This can be particularly useful where access to computers is limited. One of the carousel's workshops can have the use of a stand-alone machine or a small group of computers for a specific purpose.

It is worth mentioning here that, for those students who have them, smart-phones can act as a sort of personal carousel, enabling them to download material for use outside the classroom.

Interactive whiteboard

Differing from a traditional whiteboard by their interactivity and by the opportunities given to students to take control of their learning, these whiteboards can encourage concentration and promote interest in the activity. They are a valuable tool in the classroom and can be used, for example:

- to show something to the whole class – a grammar point, a document, a film, an image, whatever. The item is stocked on the computer and the whiteboard enables it to be seen by everyone. It can then, of course, be acted upon
- with the special pen provided with the whiteboard, to make changes to the image projected, such as altering a sentence, changing word order, adding something that wasn't there. So for grammar, syntax, vocabulary, it can make an exercise more fun
- to create from simple source material something more expanded
- to provide immediate access to authentic material, for instance film reviews, transport timetables, hotel websites, as well as to webcams for weather forecasts and all kinds of video materials such as adverts, songs and short films.

Useful software

Word-processing

It goes without saying that for all forms of written work, word-processing can be used. It is also worth stressing that it is important to emulate exam conditions at some time in the learning process by having students write by hand. This is especially important in languages where non-English characters are used, as the student must get used to forming these characters.

With most software packages, it is possible to choose your language in the options. This has benefits for spell-checking, though spelling and grammar checkers need to be used with care – they do not always react appropriately. More usefully, all word-processors have the means to "Insert/Special characters" or similar, enabling characters such as ç, à, ñ or ö to be produced. Even better, computer keyboards can be reprogrammed to produce such characters, usually using the Ctrl and/or Alt keys plus appropriate letters or the ASCII code. Naturally, students will need training in using them.

Ideas for using word-processing:

- writing CVs and job applications
- creating a portfolio of good work
- writing summaries of what you have discovered on the Internet
- completing worksheets
- working on a document collaboratively (but see below for file-sharing applications)
- taking notes
- creating a class newspaper/diary/project
- writing and illustrating stories.

Presentations and spreadsheets

Presentation packages enable students to prepare, for example:

- the results of surveys or any other information-based work
- the main points of an argument
- images to go with text, audio or video.

Spreadsheets can be used to prepare statistical analyses, or to create a database – see below.

Students can produce a PowerPoint presentation on a given topic, speaking in full sentences, *but using only bullet points*. The rest of the group can assess the performance, thus developing a deeper understanding of success criteria. This technique can also help to develop memorisation techniques using just bullet points/key words. This is the format of some assessment techniques for examinations (in the UK).

Glossaries

Many VLEs (see below) have a glossary function, which enables students to construct a joint class glossary, a kind of class vocabulary list. They can be encouraged to add items using visuals, audio, definition, sentences containing the word and translation, thus making use of the major means of encouraging vocabulary retrieval.

E-books, including downloadable periodicals and magazines

These are becoming more and more available and some devices also allow the reader to have the book read to them. It's true that the reading isn't always brilliant, but it helps students to associate sound with the written form, and there is every hope that it will improve in the future. While many classics are free to download, more recent books come with a small price, but building an e-library shouldn't break the budget.

Note: Many of the older books have been scanned in, and especially in non-English languages this can produce strange punctuation and even spelling. Spotting such errors would give students useful practice in editing!

Ideas covered in other chapters

- *Map software*: See Chapter 9, "Larger groups".

- *Video and audio websites and software*: See Chapter 13, "Action learning through pictures".

- *Images and posters*: See Chapter 13, ibid.

- *Online dictionaries and encyclopaedias*: See Chapter 18, Thesauruses and synonym dictionaries.

More complex ideas

Webquests

In another example of project-based work, a *webquest*,[1] the students collaborate to find the information they need through a defined set of Internet links – in fact, the scenario described in Chapter 9 is carried out using ICT.

For example ...   *SCENARIO → WEBQUEST...*

The scenario detailed above can easily be transformed into a webquest and a fully ICT-mediated activity. To do this:

- the assessment sheet is on the network and students write directly into the file. They save their version under their name. Their work can then be accessed by the teacher for marking

- the links to websites of adventure holiday centres and to transport sites are listed on the mission sheet and/or on the assessment sheet, so that students simply have to click on the links. These links and the site content could also be downloaded onto the school server to prevent surfing by the students outside the mission brief

- students' discussions can be recorded using a single headphone equipped with a microphone and held between them, or a stand-alone microphone. This recording can be used for follow-up work once the teacher has identified specific points needing attention or which are particularly praiseworthy.

---

[1] *WebQuest Taskonomy: A taxonomy of tasks* (B. Dodge, http://webquest.sdsu.edu/taskonomy.html, 1999).

Using and creating podcasts

Podcasts allow students to choose the space they learn in, opening classroom doors in a virtual way. Many foreign newspapers, magazines and radio stations offer ready-made podcasts, but this is also an excellent opportunity for students to make their own. Instead of a class production on paper, this could be an audio one, requiring similar skills of editing and journalism, helped by the language assistant, if your school has one. The podcasts could be stocked in the school's Intranet, making them easy to download.

Recording in examination conditions

It may be that your exam board requires oral examinations to be recorded. Recording any oral assessment makes criterion-based assessment of the performance a lot easier. In terms of formative assessment (see Chapter 4), the recordings can be accessed by students in private, making them more conscious of accent problems and of any remedial work needed. What's more, students become more used to the idea of being recorded.

Computer-mediated communication (CMC)

Webquests can be taken further through *synchronous/asynchronous* computer-based communication – i.e., Instant Messaging (IMs)/forums or blogs – that many students have experience of in their private lives. One of the main benefits is the sense of community and collaboration that is encouraged, but with both forms of CMC, you have to control both the content of messages and the selection of the respondent. Sometimes, too, some members of the group may take charge of the interaction, to the detriment of the development of skills in the other members of the group. This is less of a problem with asynchronous communication, where there is a delay between responses. This gives time for any irregularities to be picked up, and for the students to think about the form of their communication, to check vocabulary, to revise what they have written, etc.

Synchronous CMC (SCMC)

Synchronous web-based communication is very spontaneous: students correspond in real time, responding to each other's messages as soon as they receive them.

- *Chat* and *IMs* are both forms of SCMC that, if recorded, can be used for formative assessment. Of course, interaction by writing is nothing like speaking, but chatters use a very oral version of the language, albeit in code, which our students have to learn from their respondent. Alternatively, both students can use their own national code; this gives valuable practice in deciphering target language messages. Analysing such exchanges reveals requests for clarification, for unknown words, as well as recasts (where the receiver corrects and sends back the correct version) and negotiation of meaning (see Chapter 20).

- *Video-conferences* can be wonderful, but they should not be attempted in large groups, as they will become a lecture instead of an interaction. It is a good idea to have a specific theme and to prepare for the conference in advance. Most good video-conferencing software enables the sharing of documents, chat, looking at documents on the Internet, and other features. Many LEAs are experimenting with this idea, and video-conference links are being set up between schools and between regions.

Asynchronous CMC (ACMC)

Most asynchronous CMC involves writing. While chat is pretty spontaneous, forums and other forms of ACMC offer students the chance to check what they write before they post. The following are examples.

- *Emails*, despite their long history, are still invaluable for communicating with fellow-students, and especially with partner schools abroad. It is often easier to compose the message in a word-processor (that can produce accented characters more easily) before copying it across into the email.

- *Microblogs*, such as Twitter, can be a useful ICT application. The severe limit to the length of messages encourages the use of shorter synonyms for longer words, but can also make students very aware of phonetic transcriptions. "GR8" doesn't work in French! But "bjr sava?" And "keskeC" or "jeteléDjadi"? The exchanges between the two students, one NNS and one NS in each language, can be very interesting.

- *Wikis* (simple web pages that groups of friends can edit together) are wonderful for encouraging the sense of owning a document. The students are invited to contribute to a jointly constructed database. It is important to make it possible to track back the different contributions, as one student may well "correct" what another has put, and do so erroneously.

- *File-sharing applications* such as Google docs can be very helpful in group-work such as the collaborative writing of a report, or the preparation of a presentation.

- The construction of a *class blog* has its place here. A type of writing that seems less like an exercise is always welcome, and the collaboration required for a class blog can be beneficial. Good subjects for blogs include class trips, visits and exchanges, twinning events, diaries. Blogs can also be created by two classes in a partner school or even within the same institution. This gives a purpose to reading, as students want to find out what the other class/ classmates have written.

Simulated telephone conversations

Telephone conversations can most easily be simulated by linking students together in the language lab. If this is not possible, then an internal phone system can be used. Verbal communication has great advantages:

- reaction time is much faster than face to face (there is a need to fill the blank time)
- vocabulary is retrieved more speedily
- risk-taking: if the speaker can't think of a word, for example, s/he is led to take a risk by using a different formulation
- real-time working: the speaker has to react in real time and can't take the time to check anything
- realistic performance: the true abilities of the speaker can be assessed.

The Internet

The choice of Internet sites available to students should be limited, in order to prevent them from accessing undesirable material and also to avoid a massive waste of time spent trawling through the million possibilities given by a standard search engine. A good solution is to put a list on the school's Intranet, with sub-headings such as dictionaries, reference sites, pronunciation, grammar, vocabulary, letter-writing. For pronunciation, for example, these sites are useful, though there are many others:

- fonetiks:[2] different accents for nine commonly studied languages
- forvo:[3] a very complete reference for 281 languages.

By putting the sites that you authorise the students to access on the Intranet, you can more closely guide their work. However, the main advantage of the Internet is that it encourages students to take greater responsibility for their learning. It also places the target language within a context – students discover that it is used for all of the same purposes as in their own language. For the same reason, it is

---

[2] www.fonetiks.org/indexother.html
[3] http://fr.forvo.com/languages

good for them to learn the basic computing terms in the target language – though they may find a lot of English!

Virtual Learning Environments (VLEs)

Most schools will now use some form of VLE or Intranet. VLEs can be used for highly useful ICT applications, such as the following.

- *Assignment spaces*: many VLEs enable students to upload their work with a cut-off time, allowing you to collect the work virtually, correct it on your own computer and give it back to the students electronically. You can then store the work on your own computer, to have access to it at any time – useful for report writing, formative assessments, etc.

- *Databases*: uploading, and even collaboratively creating, databases for students to use is made easy.

- *Glossaries*: see above.

- *Upload*: Webquests, scenarios, projects, collaborative work, past examination papers – all of these can be delivered through the VLE. The instructions, activity or task guidelines, answer sheets, answer keys, documents or links can all be uploaded and accessed in or outside the classroom. In this way, they can promote guided autonomy in learning. The activities associated with a text can easily be differentiated, or the texts themselves can be classified by level, with the students deciding the level they want to work at.

- *Exercisers*: create an exercise easily – the students can do this too.

- *Questionnaires*: interesting for the students to make questionnaires, but also for the teacher to see what the students feel about the class.

- *Surveys*: for example, to pick a time for an appointment, or to choose the preferred name for a group or a destination for a class outing.

- *Feedback*: give feedback to the students through the VLE. Through a forum, advice can be given to students, as well as important information. With this material, you can incorporate such exercises and activities as pre-tasks for a much wider task (see scenario work above).

- Access to *listening material/video* that can be completed independently at the student's own pace, and that can vary the menus of tasks set for homework.

ICT in the languages classroom

There is a tendency to think of ICT as the panacea for language-learning ills, because it can be used for so many activities and tasks, as well as for helping students to work individually on remedial skills. However, despite its versatility, it is only one of the tools in the language teacher's toolbox. Moreover, students can get overloaded with ICT in every single school subject! Even if catastrophic breakdowns are less frequent than they used to be, ICT can go wrong, access to the VLE can go down, the Internet can go slow on you, the site that you based the webquest on can change from one day to another, etc. So it is important to have a Plan B when using this tool, just as it is with all other tools.

Despite these concerns, ICT can often give an extra buzz to other classroom activities. Its use in facilitating research and group-work and individualising learning makes it invaluable.

CHAPTER 11

Interactive communication

Interaction is one of the most important activities that promote the acquisition of language. Communicative activities have real purposes: to find information, break down barriers, talk about self, and learn about the culture. Even when a lesson is focused on developing reading or writing skills, such activities should be integrated into the lesson. Furthermore, research on second language acquisition (SLA) suggests that more learning takes place when students are engaged in relevant tasks within a dynamic learning environment rather than in traditional teacher-led classes.

The activities described below can be used successfully with many class levels. They are especially crucial for beginners' classes as vehicles to move students toward independent and confident learning. To make the activities as useful as possible, remember the following.

- Keep teacher talk to a minimum.
- Explain as much as possible by demonstrating the process, explaining in different ways, and repeating.
- Don't worry if every student doesn't understand every part of an activity. Move on when the majority of the students get the idea, and then circulate and help as needed – unobtrusively.
- One way to gauge the success of a class is to observe how much or how little the students are dependent on the teacher. The more students are working independently, in pairs, or in small groups, the more successful the class.

The following are some communicative activities that have been found to work well.[1]

---

[1] The activities are adapted with permission from National Center for Family Literacy and Center for Applied Linguistics (2008), *Practitioner Toolkit: Working with Adult English Language Learners*, Adapted with permission. Retrieved from www.cal.org/caela/tools/program_development/CombinedFiles1.pdf

Interactive communication

Class surveys

Fun and not overly challenging, these are very effective as ice-breaking activities. It is important to do something with the survey information. Otherwise, there is no intrinsic reason for gathering the information. Therefore, plan ways to process the information. Make sure the survey questions are appropriate to the class, and do not inadvertently ask about an uncomfortable topic.

Objective: Students gather information about a particular topic. They increase their proficiency and confidence in asking one or more questions, and at the same time they are improving their writing skills.

Context: A class survey activity is especially useful for beginning levels, because not much information needs to be asked for or recorded, and only one or two questions and answers need to be learned. Surveys also can be used with higher levels if more complex questions and answers are required. For example, with a beginners' class, a survey might consist of one question that simply requires students to ask and record the name of every person in class. In a more advanced class, a survey might require students to ask and record the names of television shows watched and time spent watching these shows in the past week.

You need to make a survey form so that students can easily ask the questions and record answers (see boxed example below). If the information is going to be gathered into a simple bar graph or pie chart, this needs to be ready in advance.

Procedure: Build on what students already know (e.g., the common questions, *"What's your name?"* or *"Do you have a pet? What sort is it?"*). Therefore, pre-teach and practise the questions and vocabulary needed to answer the questions.

1 Hand out the survey forms and explain the task to students.

2 Model the procedures with one or two student volunteers and check comprehension of instructions. For example, ask, "What are the questions on the survey form?" or "How many people will you talk to today?"

3 Once students begin to complete the survey, monitor the process and be ready to assist students if they ask for help.

4 Discuss the information with the class. Using the information from the surveys, you can ask questions such as, "How many of you have a dog/cat?" or "How many people watched TV more than 10 hours last week? What shows were watched the most frequently?" Students can work in groups to categorize information, create graphs or write sentences summarizing the information.

5 To add an element of cultural comparison when going through the answers, you can ask the class to consider what the answer would be in another country. For example, when talking about pets, would people living in a small village in rural Burkina Faso have a pet hamster? Why not? What about the fate of a guinea pig in Peru, where the animal is eaten?

Evaluation: Circulate and listen to the questions and answers. Collect the information sheets to look for writing weaknesses.

Learning an alphabet

Comment: Apart from being a good way to build cohesion, a survey held early in the school year asking for class-mates' names is also an excellent opportunity to start teaching the alphabet of the target language. In all facets of life people often have to spell their names or ask how something is spelled, so they need to be able to ask *"How do you spell it?"* and to understand the answer.

Put up a permanent display showing the alphabet of the target language, with "phonetic" pronunciation guides. As students spell their names and hear others spell theirs, they solidify their alphabetic knowledge. After the students have written down all the names (including their own names), there are several ways to process the information.

- You can pass out another blank list and ask students to work in pairs or small groups to alphabetise the names and then to transcribe them again in alphabetical order. As you demonstrate the process using several examples, the students are continuing to memorise their classmates' names, as well as working on the basic skill of alphabetising. Students will be much more interested in this activity than if they were asked to alphabetise a list of words that had no meaning for them.

- As an alternative, you can work through the alphabetising as a group activity at the board or on an overhead or poster.

Par exemple . . .   UN SONDAGE SIMPLE (DÉBUTANTS) . . .

Nom _____

Date _____

Instructions:

Pose les questions à chacun(e) des élèves.

Écris leurs noms.

Comment tu t'appelles ? (Comment ça s'écrit ?) **Où tu habites ?**

_____   _____

_____

_____

_____

_____

_____

_____

Conversation grid

Highlights: Conversation grid activities are a step up from a survey. The power of using them is that students are involved in authentic, independent and cooperative conversations without the teacher being directly involved. These grids can be used with any topic as teaching or assessment activities. Students usually enjoy them greatly.

Objective: Students practise and increase knowledge of language structures (such as *what?*, *when?*, *where?*, and *why?* questions and their typical answers), vocabulary (as related to a particular topic such as "My summer holiday"), and cultural aspects related to a topic. They ask questions, listen to answers, and record information on the grid.

Materials: Draw/display a large grid on the board or have an overhead transparency with a sample of the grid to explain the activity. Students need conversation grids to record answers (see boxed example below). Grids can have complete questions (e.g., *"What is your name? What do you do in your free time?"*) or cue phrases (e.g., *Name?, Hobbies?*).

Procedure:

1 Review language structures and key vocabulary that have been previously taught and are needed to complete this activity. The review should be both verbal and written, with plenty of input from the students. For example, if one of the questions is to be about hobbies, get students to suggest names of hobbies and put the target language equivalents up on the board, so that they are easily accessible when students begin to work on their own grids.

2 Hand out the grids and explain the task: "Today you're going to interview five classmates. Write their answers to your questions on this form."

3 Discuss conversation questions, e.g., *"How do you get to school? How long does it take?"*, *"What do you do in your free time? What else do you like to do?"*

4 Talk about possible answers such as *by bus/train/I walk, half an hour, play soccer, watch soccer on TV*.

5 Model the task with one or two student volunteers. It's important to model several answers and questions so that students know that full sentence answers such as *"I like playing football"* and short answers such as *"football"* are both acceptable.

Note: Modelling correct answers to issues such as *"Her name"* vs. *"She name"* is more effective than giving a big explanation about the correct grammar. This is especially true with formulaic phrases that use structures not yet discussed in class.

---

6 Check comprehension of instructions. For example, ask "How many questions are you asking each classmate?" or "How many people will you talk to today?".

7 Once students begin the activity, monitor the process and be ready to assist them if they ask for help.

> *Note*: Some will finish only one conversation while others may do several. That doesn't matter; students process, learn, and interact at different rates.

8 When the general buzz quiets down, it is time to stop the activity. Discuss the information with the class; for example, "Tell the class something you learned about one of your classmates". You can tabulate information on a master grid or have students work in small groups to do a tabulation of their grid information.

Evaluation: Evaluation is ongoing and informal. You can participate or just observe the conversations to note how well students communicate (as well as observing writing abilities from the grid). This is particularly useful, as you can watch individual students' progress from week to week.

Par exemple . . . GRILLE DE CONVERSATION: DÉTAILS PERSONNELS

Comment tu t'appelles ? (Comment ça s'écrit ?)	Quel est ton passe-temps favori ?	Et le soir, qu'est-ce que tu fais ?

Line dialogue

Highlights: This activity is good for a change of pace and gets students out of their chairs interacting with everyone in the class. A great deal of peer-teaching and friendly conversation can happen throughout this activity.

Objective: Students get intensive practice using the target language in short dialogues. They get to know one another in an atmosphere where peer-teaching is naturally supported.

Context: This activity can be used in all levels or multi-level classes. It works best for classes/groups with at least 10–12 students.

Interactive communication

Materials: Students form up in two lines, facing each other. Those in one line have *cue cards* containing questions which they will put to those in the other line. Cue cards can contain word or picture clues to responses to questions. Realia (authentic items) are also effective for beginners' classes. For higher level students, or if students are using familiar questions such as *"What is your name?"* or *"How are you?"*, cue card prompts may be unnecessary. *"What would you do if you won one million euros?"* or *"What would you like to be doing 10 years from now?"* might be questions asked and answered in a line dialogue with intermediate or advanced students.

Procedure:

1 Pre-teach the structures and lexis of the dialogue.

2 Hand out cue cards to students in Line A.

3 Line A remains stationary, repeating the same questions to every student in Line B. Students in Line B respond to the question and then move to the right and face another student in Line A. All pairs talk at once. The last person in Line B moves to the beginning of the line. The activity continues until everyone in Line A has asked everyone in Line B a question.

Example: Task: students will identify body parts from visuals.

Dialogue: A: *What's wrong?* B: *My back hurts.*

Note: There are various ways to set up a line dialogue. There may be only one line asking questions, or both lines can ask questions. As discussed above, cue cards may or may not be used. In classes where students have some familiarity with everyday language, they decide on their own what questions to ask. In all cases, one line remains stationary and the other moves.

Evaluation: This activity provides you with an excellent opportunity to evaluate students unobtrusively. Once students understand how to conduct a line dialogue, they usually have so much fun that they don't pay attention to the teacher at all. During this activity, you can observe students' speaking and listening skills, vocabulary knowledge, question formation or clarification skills, and even how comfortable they are using the target language.

Information gap

Highlights: In this activity two students share information to complete a task. In one-way gap activities, one student has all the information (e.g., one student describes a picture and the other student draws it). In two-way gap activities, both students have some information and must share it with the other to complete the task. Because this activity usually combines speaking and listening with reading and writing, all the skills are practised.

Objective: Students find and share information by asking and answering questions in order to complete a task.

Context: This activity can be used in all levels or with multi-level groups.

Materials: Prepare a master handout based on information, language structures, and vocabulary the students have been working on. Then, delete pieces of information on two sets of handouts. For example, Handout A will have some information deleted that Handout B will provide. Handout B will have other pieces of information deleted that Handout A will provide. (See boxed example below.)

You can make one side more challenging than the other, to meet the needs of students at different levels.

Procedure:

1   Pre-teach and practise vocabulary and structures for the particular task. Students should also be familiar with question and answer formulas (e.g., *"What time is __?"* and *"It's at __"*), and ways to ask for clarification (e.g., *"Excuse me, can you repeat?"*, or *"I'm sorry, I don't understand"*). These can be introduced in the early days of a class, and recycled, adapted and extended over time.

2   Explain the information-gap procedures by modelling a sample gap activity with an able volunteer from the class.

3   Have students work with a partner. One student gets Handout A and the other gets Handout B. Ask two students to model the asking and answering of questions in the gap activity, before the whole class begins the activity.

4   Ask students to compare their papers with each other.

5   To complete the activity as a whole group, you can ask volunteers to come up to the board or overhead to fill in information they've gathered from their partner. This helps solidify the knowledge and gives some slower students or pairs a chance to catch up and check their work without stress.

Evaluation: Walking around the room observing students during the activity will let you know how well individual students use and understand the target language, and how well they can read from a written text.

Variations: The handouts may be menus, advertisements, maps, pictures or charts, as well as readings.

Par exemple . . .   *INFORMATION TROUÉE BILATÉRALE . . .*

Élève A:

Lis l'histoire à ton/ta partenaire, Quand tu arrives à un blanc ____, demande de l'aide à ton/ta partenaire.

Il était une fois un petit loup qui était très sympa, mais tout le monde (1)____ qu'il était méchant, parce qu'il était un (2)____. Le loup était très triste. Il s'est assis dans la (3)____ et il s'est dit. « Il faut que je prouve que je ne suis pas (4)____, mais comment? ». À ce moment il a entendu quelqu'un qui chantait. « On n'a pas (5)____ du gros méchant loup, du gros méchant loup . . . ».
Le loup a (6)____ les chanteurs jusqu'à leurs cabanes. Il s'agissait de trois petits (7)____. Le loup a frappé à la porte d'une des cabanes. Un des cochons a (8)____ la porte. Il avait très peur, Mais le loup lui a tout expliqué.

Écoute l'histoire. Aide ton/ta partenaire avec les mots dans la liste.

1. situation
2. demandé
3. cabanes
4. attaquer
5. avec
6. mordre
7. troisième
8. intérieur

Maintenant, lis l'histoire entière à tour de rôle.

Élève B:

Écoute l'histoire. Aide ton/ta partenaire avec les mots dans la liste.

1. croyait
2. loup
3. forêt
4. méchant
5. peur
6. suivi
7. cochons
8. ouvert

Lis l'histoire à ton/ta partenaire, Quand tu arrives à un blanc ____, demande de l'aide à ton/ta partenaire.

Les cochons ont très bien compris la (1)____, et ils ont promis d'aider le loup. Ils ont (2)____ au loup de les aider à renforcer les (3)____ pour que les autres loups ne puissent plus les (4)____. On a renforcé la première cabane (5)____ du fibre de carbone, et quand les méchants loups sont venus, ils n'ont pas pu la (6)____. La deuxième cabane a été construite en béton, et les loups n'ont pas pu la démolir. La (7)____ cabane a été recouverte de miroirs, et les loups ont cru qu'il y avait d'autres loups à l'(8)____. Résultat: les cochons et le petit loup 3 points, les gros méchants loups 0 points.

Maintenant, lis l'histoire entière à tour de rôle.

Language experience approach

Highlights: The language experience approach to instruction builds students' literacy skills, as their personal experiences are transcribed and become their reading material. This is particularly valuable for beginners whose oral skills exceed their literacy skills, as spoken language and written language are linked.

A language experience story can be effective for class community building. Follow-up can include using the class-generated text to teach explicit literacy skills through activities that require students to select words from the story for exercises on vocabulary, spelling, or sound–symbol correspondence. The text can also be used to review a grammar point, such as sequence of tenses, word order, or pronouns.

Objective: To record students' own ideas and oral language and use the stories to increase literacy skills.

Context: This activity can be very effective in beginners' classes where most of the students have limited writing skills.

Procedure:

1 First, students need to share an experience, such as going to a museum, the local fair, or a supermarket. Sharing an evocative photograph or picture story or watching a video could also provide the prompt.

2 Elicit the story of the experience by asking students questions and encouraging them to contribute to the story. *Note*: Each member of the whole group can make a comment. In some groups it might be most effective to go around the room in order, assuming that all will respond. You can also ask for volunteers, and in multi-level groups the more proficient or confident students might speak first, giving the other students time to think and to form their responses.

3 Write down what students say. *Note*: There are opposing ideas about how a language experience approach activity should be conducted. Some teachers say that, to be authentic, the teacher must record exactly what each student says, even if it is not correct. Others say that a teacher should correct a student's words (e.g., by changing incorrect number, pronouns or verb form) because students want to use the target language correctly, and that writing down mistakes reinforces the mistake. The latter approach often serves the student better.

4 After recording the story, read it aloud to the group and give the students an opportunity to edit or revise (adding or eliminating information).

5 Provide students with an opportunity to read the story. They can read it in unison, or take turns reading it aloud.

6 Use the story to develop reading skills. For example, you can make sentence strips and have students put the sentences in order. To build vocabulary, you can create *Cloze* activities in which students fill in the blanks with key words.

Evaluation: The sharing of the experience and the activity itself can give you an idea about how comfortable students are feeling with the class, other students, and the topic. An individual's part of the group story can provide information about oral proficiency. You can monitor reading and writing skills as students complete follow-up activities.

Jeopardy

Highlights: The game should be played at a brisk speed, thus testing students' ability to react. *Note*: The game board shown below is assumed to be constructed manually, but it can also be programmed electronically, making it much easier to operate. The "pieces of paper" are then replaced with the money items entered electronically and so programmed that when touched they reveal the food item "hiding" beneath them. The grid can then be displayed, for example, on an inter-active whiteboard. (Programming this would be an excellent project for a student in the ICT department.)

Objective: This game gives students practice with "some/any" phrases combined with count/non-count nouns, numbers and money, followed by practice with questions such as *"How much/many?"* or *"Do we need . . .?"*.

Context: Both the subject matter and the complexity of the grid can be adjusted to suit the current topic and the students' level of knowledge.

Procedure:

1 Write/display the grid shown below on the board.

2 Cover each box with a piece of paper that has a money designation suitable for your target language; e.g., Cherries is covered with €10, Apples with €20, and so on until €50 – explain that the sums are not meant to be realistic! Covering the items ensures that students do not know which food item they will need to use in the sentence before they make their selection.

3 The student says, for example, "I'd like some fruit at €. . .". The relevant slot is then uncovered and s/he must continue by asking any question about the item revealed, such as "Have you any . . .?" or "How much are the . . .?".

4 If the question is correctly formed, that student has another turn, but must use a <u>different</u> question next time. If the question is not correctly formed, the turn passes to the next in line.

Evaluation: As the subject matter of the grid will relate to the current topic, you can assess students' knowledge of the relevant vocabulary and phrasing, as well as their ability to form correct statements and questions under pressure.

Sample game board

Fruit	Vegetables	Meat	Dairy products	Groceries
Cherries	Onion	Fish	Yoghurt	Pasta
Apples	Beans	Turkey	Milk	Rice
Grapes	Cabbage	Beef	Butter	Sugar
Oranges	Potatoes	Chicken	Ice cream	Bread
Bananas	Tomatoes	Sausage(s)	Cheese	Flour

The 'fish-bowl'

Highlight: This is a combination of group-work with whole-class/whole-group participation.

Objective: To practise and assess the students' ability to listen closely and understand the general run of a conversation, and to intervene appropriately.

Context: This activity works very well with older students with a fair command of the language. It is very suitable for the sixth form, but can be used with Key Stage 4 students if the topic is well known to them and well prepared.

Procedure:

1 The class sits in a circle, with four chairs in the middle. (If the class is large, form sub-groups.)

2 Three students have prepared to lead the discussion, sharing out roles as they wish. These three sit in the middle; the other chair is vacant.

3 The members of the lead group start the discussion, but at any time one of the listeners in the circle can come and sit on the vacant chair, which indicates that s/he wants to ask a question or make a comment.

4 At this point, the lead group stops talking, the visitor speaks and the group deals with the point s/he is making.

5 Once this is done, the visitor goes back to the circle and the main discussion continues until another visitor arrives.

6 The audience can take notes (in the target language, of course); this helps with intervention and with the written report, if this is required.

7 The activity is usually self-limiting – it becomes clear when the three speakers have exhausted what they have to say. Another three speakers can then take over.

Evaluation: Although some students will have played a much more active role than others, all are expected to have grasped the main points of the discussion, and this can be tested by questions directed mainly at those who have been more passive. "Did the speakers have differing viewpoints?", "What was the point made by XXX when s/he intervened?", etc. Advanced classes can be asked to write a short report of the conversation.

The activities in this chapter have been presented in a way that is different from that in other chapters. However, you don't need to swallow each activity whole; some contain very familiar material (e.g., the surveys), and all contain elements that can be taken out and used separately (e.g., the question and answer series in the line dialogue activity). If you do decide to use an activity whole, prepare students well for the structures and vocabulary they will need, and take it briskly.

Drama and role-play

The main distinction between drama and role-play is in the extent to which students use their initiative and imagination: role-play is largely *practice* of known language, whereas drama involves invention and more spontaneous *use*. Both have their place in language learning.

Role-play

Role-play is clearly important as a simple type of interaction, particularly because it develops various skills, such as recognising another person's perspective and acting on it, negotiating meaning between two (or more) players, rephrasing in cases of incomprehension, and dealing with spoken information. It also has the advantage that it encourages questions as well as requiring answers, so the student is much more in control than in many other, more teacher-directed, activities.

Role-play can take many forms.

- *Problem-solving*: client and seller/employee/professional/ . . . For example, a client wants something, the employee solves the problem, proposes solutions; the client chooses the solution that most corresponds to her/his needs. This can be made more complicated and more like real life if:
  - there is no easy solution and therefore compromise is necessary on the client's part
  - some additional information is given to one side or the other halfway through; e.g., there is a strike called for that day so no trains running, a volcano has erupted in Iceland so no flights are running, the client has forgotten his credit card, the (mobile) phone rings and some important info is given to one side or the other, etc.
  - the employee is on work experience and has to keep consulting a third person to confirm what s/he's saying: s/he could, for example, get something wrong and have to correct it.

- *Simple transactional tasks* such as arranging to meet, ordering a meal in a restaurant, asking about train/flight times.

- *Mediation tasks*: one person is misunderstood by the other, who needs to rephrase. This is a strategy that is very often overlooked.

- *Persuasion*: getting someone to do something s/he doesn't want to do is highly likely to provoke reformulation by the students on both sides of the role-play. Again, this is a very valuable strategy in encouraging learning.

Much of the pair- and group-work suggested in Chapters 8 and 9 can easily develop into role-play practising a specific set of structures. For example: A has a problem, B gives advice. In the boxed examples below the focus is on various modal verbs and, especially in Germanic languages, the associated word-order. Suitable models can be rehearsed and/or displayed on the whiteboard.

Par exemple . . .   *JE PEUX T'AIDER ? . . .*

A: Je <u>veux</u> aller au disco ce soir, mais je ne <u>peux</u> pas. Je n'ai pas d'argent.

B: Tu <u>devrais/pourrais</u> demander à tes parents de te le donner.

A: Ah non! Ils ne <u>voudraient</u> pas, j'en suis certain. Ils ne <u>veulent</u> pas que je m'amuse.

B: OK! Je sais ce que tu <u>veux</u>! Je <u>peux</u> te l'emprunter – mais ça s'appelle reviens, d'accord ?

Zum Beispiel . . .   *WIE KANN ICH HELFEN? . . .*

A: Ich <u>möchte</u> heute abend in die Disko <u>gehen</u>, aber ich <u>kann</u> nicht. Ich hab' kein Geld.

B: Du <u>solltest</u> / <u>könntest</u> deine Eltern darum <u>bitten</u>.

A: Ach nein! Sie <u>würden</u> nicht <u>rausrücken</u>. Sie <u>wollen</u> mir nie <u>helfen</u>!

B: OK! Ich versteh, du <u>willst</u> bei mir <u>schnorren</u>! Also gut, ich <u>kann</u>'s dir <u>leihen</u> – aber **leihen**, hörst du, nicht **geben**!

Por ejemplo . . .   *¿PUEDO AYUDARTE?. . .*

A: <u>Quisiera</u> invitar a mi amiga a cenar, pero no <u>puedo</u> – a mis padres no se la gusta.

B: <u>Podrías</u> / <u>Deberías</u> invitarla a un restaurante.

A: No <u>puedo</u> – no tengo dinero.

B: ¿Por qué me miras así? ¡Ah! ¡Ya veo! <u>Quieres</u> que te lo preste. Pues bien, <u>puedo</u> hacerlo, ¡pero **prestar** no significa **dar**! ¡<u>Tienes que</u> devolverlo!

Peer- and auto-assessment of role-plays

If a third role-play card is prepared, with standard answers plus a few variations, then the third student can assess the performance of the others. This can encourage them to notice difficulties and again lead to negotiating meaning as well as providing scaffolding to help the players, all important elements in the language-learning process.

Drama

Especially when the topic has already been studied, perhaps under a different format, drama work is easier for you to control and for the students to enact if done in groups. The suggestions below assume this. With a little forethought, some groups can rehearse in spaces outside your classroom. It will be well worth while cooperating with the drama department; its techniques for learning lines can easily be adapted for use in the MFL department.

Setting it up

- Have clear signals for stopping and starting.
- State that no physical contact is allowed between participants.
- Use simple props or clothing to indicate roles and places, making sure that all students understand them. For example, a paper képi for a policeman; chairs facing backwards for cars.
- Tell the groups that they must continue in role until you tell them to stop, whether or not they have completed the exercise. This forces them to continue beyond the initial limits of the drama.

Deciding on the subject

As in "real life", the subject for drama may have many different sources.

- *A text previously worked on* in another format. For more advanced students, this text may very well come from a play or novella they are studying, allowing them to "tweak" the plot to produce an alternative ending. Equally, it could come from a cultural element the class has been studying.
- *A report* culled from a local newspaper or, still better, from a regional newspaper in the target language. Both of these will offer opportunities for cultural learning, but the latter adds to students' knowledge of the country whose language they are studying, as well as providing a rich source of vocabulary and phraseology to be used in the drama.

- A factual or fictional *item seen on television or in a film* the class has seen. If the film was in English, the student can play a mediator role (explaining an English film for a non-English speaker), again a valuable strategy in language-learning. This applies equally to a film in any language other than the target language, providing an opportunity for valuing other cultures.

- An event or debate in *the life of the school*. This too is the language learner as mediator. "It's happening in my school and I thought you'd like to know about it."

- Especially with less able linguists, set limits to their imagination, and keep the parameters clear, e.g., *We were all waiting to be served in a shop when* . . .

Working out the plot and allocating roles

These two tasks may appear different, but in fact they are very closely linked. Stress to students that this is *their* plot, to be changed as they think fit. As the twists of the plot are worked out, new characters will emerge, and their roles must be allocated. Conversely, the strengths and weaknesses of each participant will often determine the nature and actions of newly invented characters.

The boxed example below picks up the end of the "diamond-shaped" lesson in Chapter 3.

- *The main lines of the plot.* The source of the drama will supply the main scenes, which participants alter and add to ad lib. Roles are allocated and the relevant characters work out how each scene runs. (This is where English is most likely to be used.)

- *Producing the script.* It is not necessary to produce a finished script. Rather, once each character's role has been decided, all characters should produce a series of prompt-cards outlining their attitudes and actions in the plot. This is a crucial part of the preparation, because it eliminates the tendency to read out a written script and encourages experimentation and risk-taking.

- *Rehearsing.* Scene by scene, players fill out the dialogue, using just their cards. The same cards can then be used, if needed, in *Performance*.

Par exemple . . .	UN INCONNU ARRIVE . . .
Prof:	Pour terminer vous allez construire un drame sur la base de l'histoire que nous avons étudiée. Formez vos groupes de 6/7. Vous choisirez vos rôles, vous discuterez des détails de l'intrigue de votre drame, et puis vous noterez ce que votre personnage va dire – je vous donne cette dernière tâche pour vos devoirs. Bon, allez-y !

> *(Les membres du Groupe 1 décident des rôles qu'ils vont prendre, mais ils sont 7 et il n'y a que 6 rôles.)*
>
> **Jack:** Et moi? Il n'y a plus de rôles, qu'est-ce que je ferai?
>
> **Ava:** Il faut en inventer un. Quel rôle veux-tu jouer?
>
> **Jack:** Euh … je crois, un agent en civil.
>
> *(Le Groupe décide des détails de l'intrigue. Le prof circule. Puis, à la maison, chacun se fait sa pense-bête contenant les phrases essentielles de son rôle. Le lendemain: La famille Lebrun discute (sans se mettre d'accord) de ce qu'il faut faire de l'argent que le père de famille aura gagné au loto. Soudain, un coup de sonnette. La mère ouvre.)*
>
> **Inconnu:** Bonjour Madame. Je suis employé de la compagnie *LotoSécure* – voici ma carte. Je regrette d'avoir à vous dire que, en raison de problèmes de l'ordinateur, il faut maintenant contrôler à la main tous les tickets Loto. Veuillez me montrer le vôtre, s'il vous plaît … Ah, encore un! Je regrette, Madame, mais je dois retenir votre ticket pour le moment – veuillez signer ici ……
>
> **Agent:** Pas si vite, mon ami … enfin je vous ai! Madame, permettez que je vous présente Gobo Gobin, petit criminel que je cherche depuis longtemps. Allons, Gobo, pas d'histoires! Le fourgon attend!
>
> *Ils partent ensemble et tournent le coin, quand l'agent dit:*
>
> **Agent:** Tu as toujours le ticket, Gobo ? Bravo ! Allons encaisser!

Using video-recording equipment

Many of your students will be familiar with devices that record videos, whether they use the now old-fashioned camcorder, or their mobile phone video app, or a "Flip"-style recorder (a very small hand-held high-definition film camera that slots into the USB port of the computer for charging and downloading). These latter devices are extremely useful because of their compact size and the unobtrusive nature of the filming, although permission should of course always be sought before filming children. You can safely allow students to be director, camera operator, etc. The prospect of being "on TV" almost always adds quality to drama work, and the results can be used like any other video. Links could be forged with the technology department, for example if sound effects, a working model or any other props are required. The ICT department could help with editing the video. The camera-shy may need encouragement and reassurance, and having a role behind the camera can encourage them to come out into the limelight. Shyer students can do voice-overs off camera, for example, or wear masks if the video calls for it. This can be especially good if the task involves them pretending to be someone famous.

Among other ideas for small videos are the following.

- A school twinning situation: film family/school/class/outside school life and post it on the blog, or use it for video conferences.

- Imagine that you have to counsel someone as to the options they have to make and make a brief video extolling the virtues of biology, sport science, or any other subject.

- Prepare a presentation (an extended monologue) and then peer- and self-assess the result. Remarks will also focus on body language.

- Video a group talk or other event (see Chapter 5, and below).

"Witness statements": Video-recorders can also be used for what could be called "reverse drama": the script is settled beforehand and the challenge to the students is to report on what happens. This provides an excellent incentive to watch and listen carefully. At the end, you could reveal that research has shown that accounts by witnesses in real life are very often not at all accurate!

Either individually for homework or perhaps in groups, students write a script for a brief action-packed scene, including indications of costume, small props and stage-directions. It is important that the scenes should be no longer than 10 to 15 seconds, with plenty of action and speech but few characters.

- You take them all in for correction and select one or two for videoing.

- The roles in the selected scene(s) are allotted and the scene is rehearsed and finally videoed, out of sight of the class. The participants are instructed not to reveal any details of the plot.

- The class is warned to watch carefully and the scene is run, possibly twice (to make it easier).

- The watching students then either write a brief "witness statement" (harder) or answer set "interview" questions (easier). The students' reports/answers to the questions can be on any aspect of the scene, including the correctness of the language.

- Finally, the scene is run again, perhaps with pauses, while the students check their own accounts or their partner's.

This activity can equally well be run "live", i.e., without videoing the scene. The process is the same, except that this time the "actors", having rehearsed privately, are instructed to burst into the classroom at a given point without warning, enact the scene and rush out again. It doesn't matter if one of them "fluffs" her/his lines; the group must hurry on regardless. Indeed, this challenges the audience to spot such errors and comment on them. For checking, the scene can be videoed as it happens, but if not, the script could be photographed and displayed – not that this guarantees that it shows what actually occurred.

Drama and role-play

A prime educative value in both versions is when students compare their own account with their partner's; this usually demonstrates how unreliable witness statements can be.

Remember: In many of these activities, with or without video, students will find it hard to express themselves in the target language and will fall back on English. You can limit this by ensuring that they are well prepared and by circulating and supplying them with the necessary target language expressions, which they can note down and learn. Success in this stage of the activity depends very much on your support and on regular training.

CHAPTER 13

Exploiting audio and video texts

The relative ease with which audio and video materials can be used makes them very suitable for interactive activities. The viewer can interact with both image- and sound-based text, and can explore it, study it, play within it. In common with efficient reading of a text, and to use that as a metaphor, the pause button gives the viewer time to look up from the "page" and reflect on what's just been "read", before picking up where s/he left off. If this interaction is managed by the teacher, then the whole class or group can do the same thing.

Using audio and video documents in the classroom involves working with the medium that delivers the language. The language is the content of the document, as it is in a written text, but the medium delivering it is different, and the language itself changes because of the chosen medium. Video requires fine comprehension: meaning is conveyed as much through the visual as through the words, while audio-only documents tend to be more explicit.

It is important to integrate videos into your teaching plan, not to regard them just as "fun extras". The most difficult challenge is finding suitable television and film for use in the classroom, in terms of language, of course, but especially in terms of interest and run time. Adverts can be very useful, particularly if a product is sold both in the country of the target language and in the first-language country, since comparing the varying treatment of the product can give insight into the traditions or culture of each country.[1] News reports and excerpts from long films can be useful too. Three minutes is a manageable run time in most circumstances, though much shorter excerpts are often better for intensive work.

---

[1] A perfect example of this occurred when a well-known ice-cream advert ended with a regretful "What a pity there's never enough XXX!". However, when this advert was to be shown in the Middle East, a marketing specialist pointed out that you couldn't possibly imply that a middle-class Arab housewife had run out of anything. So the final text was changed to "How lucky we have a freezer full of XXX!".

Pre-recorded audio and video

Authentic audio recordings of native speakers talking are very valuable, but they are often used for testing *à la GCSE* rather than for teaching and learning. Not only this, but unless the individual results of these tests are recorded, students do not discover what they can and cannot yet do, and nor do you.

Give students as much opportunity as possible to listen to recordings by themselves or (better) in small groups. This means having more recorders, setting up carousels of activities (see Chapter 2, "Carousel working"), or using the VLE of your school. Alternatively, if you have the right to put the recordings onto MP3 players, individual students can download the MP3 onto their MP3 players. Any of these methods allows students to re-run passages, making some tasks possible that would otherwise be very hard.

Pre-listening

Encourage students to predict the content of the passage that they are about to hear. Do this by:

- using visual clues to help comprehension
- giving the title of the whole passage or of each section and encouraging speculation
- giving information about the speaker – news reporters usually give background information about interviewees to help listeners identify the coming point of view
- writing up certain words or phrases. On the first playing students simply tick the words as they hear them. This can be turned into a team game by having two volunteers from two teams race to tick off the relevant item. By picking out more difficult words and phrases you can help students not to regard the unknown as mere noise
- listing questions in TL: individually or in teams, as above, students tick when they think they have heard the answer. This is a form of gist listening that, by concentrating attention on what is relevant, helps to inculcate in the student an awareness of redundancy
- reading out unknown words so that they are more recognisable. This can also reinforce the differences in the pronunciation of similar words in English and the target language.

Many of these techniques also help to inculcate the idea that it is not essential to understand every word to grasp the meaning of the whole.

Listening for later production

Here students have to identify, then re-use for their own purposes, the language they hear. "Own purposes" implies substituting certain elements for others, making it essential to identify the basic phrase. Techniques mentioned above can be adapted by putting the phrases on the board in the wrong order, to be identified, reordered and then adapted for productive use.

Some types of exploitation

These examples are of *very* approximate levels of difficulty (marked A to D). Many are a form of gist listening that, by concentrating attention on what is relevant, helps to develop the student's awareness of what is irrelevant. For some exercises, students can fill in a grid. Or they can match lists (names against statements, two halves of sentences, etc.). Many of these exercises can be adapted for written texts (see Chapter 14).

[A] Students make a tick whenever they hear one or more defined *words* or sounds (*emphasis on discrimination and detail*). [C] The words can be of a given subject or type (see below). By picking out more difficult words and phrases you help students not to regard the unknown as mere noise.

[A] From a numbered list of phrases/sentences, students write down the number of any *phrase* heard on the recording (*ditto*) – not all the listed phrases are actually on the recording.

[A] Students assess what *time* the passage is talking about. The present/past/future? What were the clues?

[B] From what they hear on the recording, students fill in *blanks* in a list of phrases (*ditto + spelling*).

[B] Students write "✓/✗" for each of a numbered list of spoken *statements* about the recording.

[B] Recapitulate a *sequence* in the whole class or groups, using key words and other means of support.

[B] Aural/grammatical *discrimination* (see Chapter 6, "Hearing the difference") – *Lequel as-tu entendu: « vous » ou « vu » ?*

[C] Turn down the *sound* of a video and get students to provide the dialogue – support by using the pause and re-run buttons.

[C] List various *questions* on the text in the target language: individually or in teams, as above, students tick when they think they have heard the answer.

Audio and video texts

[C] Students note down any *useful phrases* and use them in their pair/group discussions, written work, etc. (*emphasis on meaning + integration of skills*). This is good stuff for differentiation.

[C] Students note down the *key words* in a sentence/passage. What is their meaning?

[C] Stop recording and ask *Qu'est-ce qu'elle/il a dit ?* – exact reproduction not required (*incentive to listen, emphasis on pronunciation/intonation/meaning*).

[C] Play a short section several times (students perhaps repeating), then stop recording and ask *Qu'est-ce qu'elle/il va dire?* (*emphasis on meaning and prediction*).

[C] Students pick out specific short pieces of *information* from the recording.

[C] Students write answers to open-ended *questions* about the recording.

[D] Give students a single word from each of a series of recorded *sentences* and ask them to say or note down which words "go with" them – for example, adjective + noun, subject + verb + object (*emphasis on structure*).

[D] Where the topic is suitable, students note down any words they hear of a certain *type* (noun, adjective, verb, adverb – *emphasis on structure*) or on a given *topic* (part of body, food and drink – *emphasis on meaning*), etc. [B] They can also just tick, then compare the number(s) heard. (This can be done in two teams: "Raise your hand if you think you have heard a word. *You must then say it* – plus point if you can, minus point if you can't.")

[D] Students listen for specific structures, for example:

- Which question does this sentence answer – *When? Where? How?* How many words answer the question *When? Where?* Which words are they?
- How many verbs in this passage are using *être/sein* / . . . to form the perfect? Which are they? Why do they use *être/sein* / . . .?
- (*German*) How many sentences have the subject before the main verb? What other sorts of words or phrases may come before the verb? What questions do the words before the verb answer?

[D] It is usually too hard for students to write down *opinions* expressed on the recording as it runs, but [B] they can select from a numbered list of contrasting opinions. Afterwards these can be discussed, supported by any notes they have made.

There are advantages to using both commercially recorded material and authentic recordings. The former are likely to be more useful for introducing and reinforcing specific structures or lexis, while the latter provide practice in understanding and interpreting native speakers, as well as giving valuable insights into a national culture and attitudes.

A third possibility is to record your own audio documents. Several software programmes, many of them free (for example the sound editor Audacity[2]), enable you to do this. The same software can be used by students to monitor their own speech. It can also be used for recording free radio from the Internet. Your school's VLE can undoubtedly be used for making the resulting audio and video available for use by students.

Other ideas on using films/adverts

Freeze frame

- Take a frame from an advert, one that you have chosen beforehand for its relevance, poignancy, interest of any kind.

- Brainstorm the product concerned. (This could also, of course, be used for static images; see Chapter 14.)

- Bring together all the possibilities using the structures « *Il pourrait s'agir de . . .* », « *Je pense que c'est pour . . .* », « *. . . parce que. . .* ».

- Then play the advert from the beginning to the freeze frame, pause and discuss whether the hypotheses were correct, which was closest, etc. Or continue from the freeze frame and do the same.

- Then play the whole advert.

- With students of a good ability, have each group take one hypothesis and play it as in *Call My Bluff*, with each group pretending their hypothesis is the good one. You then reveal the true version by playing the advert.

Convince me

- Hold a brainstorming pre-activity in which students list the films they've recently seen, and write these up. You could do this silently, with the groups giving you a slip of paper listing their films (if you had a very noisy group this could work to calm them before the task itself). Or you could do this by everyone shouting out, so that the students can't memorise who had said what (this could be good for that very quiet group).

- Students choose one of the films they haven't seen, then mill around trying to find out who saw the film, what it was all about, who the actors were, a mini-synopsis of the film, etc. You may want to pre-teach or revise some essential structures, or you may want the students to tell you during or after the task what structures or lexis they needed. You then have an on-the-spot, on-demand focus on form.

---

[2] http://audacity.sourceforge.net

Audio and video texts

- At the end of a milling time, have the students tell you which film they chose, who had seen it and a recap of the information they found. The students naturally fall into story-telling mode as they exchange information, and each conversation is different.

Briefing the absentees

- Again, a story-telling type task. Where a longer film is being watched over several lessons, at the start of each lesson have someone recap briefly, whether anyone has been absent or not. This could be done in groups, where all students try to remember what happened last time, to consolidate their memories and to re-use the lexis and structures seen.

- Likewise, some cultural element may have struck them. This can also be done with adverts, if you are watching a series of adverts.

Focus on the music

Given that many films and adverts begin with sound, this can make a very sensory lesson.

- Set the scene by making the room as dark as possible. (If you are able to, move the classroom furniture to resemble a cinema.) Make the whole task into a fantasy: have them close their eyes and imagine themselves in the cinema, settling down in the dark, waiting for the film to begin, asking the tall guy in front to sit lower in his seat, etc.

- Tell them the film is about to start and they will hear the beginning. Ask them to concentrate on the images that the music/soundtrack brings to mind. How much of the movie can they conjure up just by listening to the soundtrack? People? Places? Colours? Feelings? Genre?

- Bring the students back to reality and have them discuss their impressions in small groups.

- In a plenary session, briefly summarise these hypotheses before putting them out of their misery by playing the musical excerpt again. This technique helps the students to concentrate on the non-linguistic stimuli that exist in real life.

- NOTA BENE: The choice of film and soundtrack is clearly of extra importance here – not all films work well. If viewing an entire film is problematic due to time constraints, a wide range of short films is available for exploitation.

Can you guess what I can see?

- Have one student or a small group watch the video extract, while the others can only hear it playing.

● Those who cannot see the extract write down what they think is happening: *Who? What? Where? When? Why? What for?* Then have them question those who have seen it in order to check if they were right.

It may have struck you that using audio and video texts in your lessons risks similar problems to using ICT (Chapter 10). You are introducing an electronic medium that you need to control carefully while at the same time basing your activities on its reliable functioning. Also, students' previous experience and therefore present expectations may be very different from yours. The solution, as always, is to make sure that they are thoroughly familiar with these media by training them progressively in their use ...

...AND THAT FROM AS EARLY AS POSSIBLE.

CHAPTER 14

Exploiting [A] texts and [B] pictures

(See also some of Chapter 13, and many examples in Chapter 9.)

In many ways, a picture is much more flexible than a text, especially if projected in the classroom. The subject portrayed can relate to the current topic, to help with descriptive vocabulary. The level of difficulty can be easily adjusted by the support given, and the picture can be switched on and off as needed. (See photo and suggested exploitation in the boxed example below. Try to use a private photo, as this one is, to avoid possible problems of copyright.)

Set exercises

Most of these activities are suitable for work in PAIRS or GROUPS, or can lead to it. Some are suitable for ICT use. Almost all can prompt the question *"Why do you think that?".* 1/2/3 = *Approximate levels of challenge.*

Short set answers

[1] [A/B] Select from multiple-choice answers to set questions.

[1] [A] Note down *any* remembered words and phrases – auto-differentiation.

[1] [A/B] Identify *True/False* statements.

[2] [A] Find/list/count words/phrases illustrating given usages/structures/topics/sounds . . .

[2] [A/B] Identify people/things from descriptions given.

[2] [A/B] Select words from a list to express a view.

[2/3] [A] Find certain information in texts, perhaps with time limit.

[2/3] [A] Pick out words in text from given synonyms, definitions, etc.

[3] [A] Underline/list key words in texts – can lead to discussion or writing.

[3] [A] Scan to extract information and record it.

Longer set answers

[1] [A] Look up words underlined in text/listed/chosen by them/ . . .

[1] [A] Look up cognates in text – *faux amis?*

[2/3] [A] Skim for general meaning; pick out main points.

[3] [A] Provide clues/definitions to words, then challenge partners.

Matching/sorting

[1] [A] Jigsaw reading ("text salad") – piece text fragments together.

[1/2] [A] Sort lists, by order in text, by importance to the student, by . . .

[3] [A/B] Compare/match two elements – two lists, pictures with captions, halves of sentences, names with statements . . .

Open-ended tasks

These tasks call for greater use of a student's initiative and imagination.

Free speech and writing

[1/2] [A/B] Write <u>any</u> statements about the text/picture – partner(s) can check.

[1/2] [A/B] Ask and answer questions on a text/picture.

[1/3] [A] Change details; write a parallel text.

[2] [A/B] Make notes, especially for other purposes.

[2] [A/B] Infer information not directly given.

[2/3] [A] Complete/continue/summarise a document.

[2] [A/B] Write sentences/pieces that practise given structures.

[2] [A] Spot the differences in conflicting reports of an event, descriptions of a scene . . .

[2/3] [B] View an image for, say, 30 seconds, answer questions on it/write an account of what was in it. (See photo and box below.)

[3] [A] Write questions for partner about structures/syntax/vocabulary of a text.

[3] [A/B] Write from prompts (questions or key words, contents of a help box, etc.) to produce opinions, (re-)narrations, descriptions, personalised versions, etc.

[3] [A] Assume various roles and re-narrate.

[3] [A] Rewrite in another format (e.g., prose to drama, picture-strip to news report).

Texts and pictures

[3] [A] Plan new document, story-line, picture-strip . . .

[3] [B] Find an interesting picture/cartoon/photograph/painting that will need the use of certain structures or vocabulary. Have students sit back to back. One student has the picture and must describe it to her/his partner, who draws it. This involves visual perception as well as using prepositions, adjectives, adverbs, and forms of the present tense. It also involves trying to find a word you don't know: *"C'est un truc qu'on utilise pour casser les noix."*

[3] [B] Again using such pictures, this time choose one that clearly implies a story before, during and after the scene shown. Students collaborate to imagine the story. You could do this with just one picture for the whole class and then vote for the best story. (See also Chapter 16, "Creating a story".)

Figure 14.1 Sample photo for exercise

Vous avez 30 secondes pour regarder cette photo – qu'est-ce que vous y voyez ? . . . OK:

[3] Prenez vos cahiers et décrivez tout ce que vous savez de la scène. Vous avez 5 minutes.

[2] Répondez aux questions sur votre feuille:

Ça se passe dans quel pays ? Pourquoi le crois-tu ? Quel temps fait-il ? Comment le sais-tu ? Tu vois combien de personnes ? Qu'est-ce qu'ils font ? L'homme à droite, où va-t-il ? Et l'homme à gauche, qu'est-ce qu'il fait ? Pourquoi y a-t-il des bateaux ? . . . . . .

Action learning through pictures

Using pictures with students is a form of action learning. How many of your students describe pictures on a daily basis? Lots!

Preparatory

1 Have students list the ways in which they encounter pictures and talk about them – if they run out of ideas, mention tabloid journalism, magazines, cartoons and story books, film. Now, you need to work on their interpretation of the images.

2 Bring in a picture that tells a thousand different stories.

3 Put the students into small groups to discuss their reactions, using the standard questions *Who?*, *What?*, *Why?*, *When?* etc., but inviting them to build the start of a story.

4 Bring the class back together and have them relate their story-board. Make this as oral as possible, avoiding giving way to any request to write it all up before speaking.

Stage 2

This could be a full-scale task, with the pre-tasks being the discussion and the search for appropriate language, and the initial preparation the election of a spokesperson to relate the story, etc. The main task will be the final telling.

1 Take in a fairly well known, current, film poster, having removed all the words. Have them name the film and the actors, what happens, etc.

2 Then ask if they'd have chosen a different image to illustrate the action of the film. Did the image accurately represent the film?

3 Have a stock of "major events" images. These could be famous sports events, famous music events, famous disasters ... Clearly, this will trigger the use of past tenses, just for the description. If you want to make it a little less "standard", ask the groups who in their family might remember a particular event.

4 Homework could then be to find out if that person remembers the event and, the next lesson, to recount what the memories were.

5 Split the class into four groups. Give each group a set of seven/eight different portraits of people. (Choose the pictures to reflect the context you've chosen.)

6 Each student chooses one of the pictures. Tell them s/he is to become the person s/he chose. Students must build up, on their own, their character (name, age, profession, residence, likes, dislikes, etc.).

7 Now have them improvise meeting the other characters in a given *context*, e.g. first day at a new school, moving into a new home, sitting on a train/bus

that has broken down and waiting for rescue . . . and in a given *place*, e.g. 20 miles south of Calais, in a rural town in the Périgord . . . After a set preparation time, they perform.

8 Take a portrait that is open to many interpretations. Then ask:

- the age of the person (there will be many different answers!)
- the language s/he might be speaking. Most students will choose either their L1 or the L2 they are learning (after all, why else might the teacher ask them to do this activity?!). But equally, s/he might be an asylum seeker, a refugee, a person rescued from a shipwreck . . .
- the manner of speaking (scared, anxious, worried, frustrated, calm . . .)
- the actions implicit in the person's stance (maybe frowning, maybe open-mouthed, maybe wide-eyed . . .).

Stage 3

These extensions can apply to most of the ideas mentioned in Stage 2, but have been specifically developed for number 1.

1 As above, but this time give the students a role to play – with names if possible and a few details about their role.

2 In their mini-groups, one of them plays the role of the person in the picture, the other two are customs officials/police/social worker/employer . . . (use your imagination to create several).

3 Maybe place the image in a context (a small port in Italy – where there are lots of refugees/asylum seekers/a shipwreck – or a port such as Calais or Marseilles in France . . .).

4 Now the task has changed radically: the choice of the role "situates" the action. The members of the group become real actors. If the person is a refugee/asylum seeker/rescued person, s/he may very well not understand the language, and therefore one student can play the role of interpreter.

5 There may be a role for a mediator between the person in the image and the authorities.

6 Choose a theme that most students in the class can identify with and for which there are websites that are acceptable for their age group. (Particularly useful with older students, but involves more work for you as you have to identify the websites.)

7 Have them look at the layout of the page, at the images used, the fonts, the colours, etc.

Both Stages 2 and 3 open students' eyes to the idea of many possible interpretations. A written extension would be to create a screenplay out of the imagined dialogue.

All this work on interpreting pictures will lead the students away from the "describe a picture" exercise, which tends to be sterile, without very much context or interest. Stage 3 above, with its addition of roles and situations, links clearly to scenario work (see Chapter 9).

An evident difference between working with a text and working with a picture is that the former will supply much of the vocabulary, and perhaps even the structures, needed to carry out the activity, whereas the latter places a much greater onus on the student to produce the necessary language. With a text, there is always the danger that the student may be able to pick out the correct answer simply by scanning the print – one of the authors once met a boy who had rightly identified "wheat" as a "cereal" but had no idea what a "cereal" was. Faced with a picture, on the other hand, a student may be quite at a loss through not knowing essential words. With a text, therefore, you should ensure that students grasp the general gist of the passage, as well as the meaning of key words, while with a picture the main thing is to prepare the vocabulary.

CHAPTER 15

Excerpts or independent reading?

We all assume that we know what is meant by "reading", but reading a book is very different from reading a short text. The book will tell a story or convey information (*fiction/non-fiction*); the much briefer texts presented to language learners may do the same, but their prime purpose is usually to instruct or to assess. We shall examine each form in the order normally experienced by students.

Working with short excerpts

Key Stage 4 content is banal ... There is a general lack of good text-based work.[1] Could there be a link between these two statements?

> It seems to me to be very important that learners recall as much as possible of a text. We learn a language mainly, some people would say entirely, from the language that we process for meaning. We learn by engaging with texts and processing them for meaning, and from seeing the way texts are put together. So it is very important for learners to make the most of the texts they have worked with. They should not simply put them on one side and forget them.[2]

Developing reading skills

Asking the students what strategies they use to understand a text can be particularly fruitful, allowing you to make sure they understand the classic sequence presented below [*]. It also gives you the opportunity to remind them how to use dictionaries successfully, while recognising their limitations. The same is even more relevant to using Internet reference sites. (See also Chapter 18, especially the "Reading" sub-section of "Using dictionaries".)

---

[1] NALA *Update* Spring 2002: summary of CILT/NALA KS4 Colloquium.
[2] Dave Willis, *Techniques for priming and recycling*, British Council/BBC, 24 April 2008: www.teachingenglish.org.uk/think/articles/techniques-priming-recycling

[*] The following sequence may be useful to students. If necessary, adapt it to suit.

i.   Study the layout of the text: title, length, pictures, typeface.

ii.   Make predictions about the contents and the function of the text.

iii. Anticipate where you will find confirmation of these predictions.

iv.   Skim-read the passage, looking for confirmation.

v.   Confirm or revise the predictions made in (ii).

vi.   Predict further.

vii. Read further and deeper in order to confirm or revise (vi).

Other useful strategies for coping with new words include the following.

- A student may suggest using context. You can then discuss how context can help you guess – and we all know how important guessing is in learning languages.

- In group work, students may make use of mime, as well as synonyms, antonyms or homonyms to show their partners the meaning of a new word.

- Word maps and word families can be drawn up and used in form-focused sessions.

This whole discussion can lead to a greater awareness and use of these strategies, which can be reinforced by exercises using one of them. Instead of just writing down a new word and its translation without context, students will be encouraged to use a variety of approaches, all of which increase the chance of their retaining the word.

Responses to texts

These are some of the techniques you can use both to help students understand a text and to assess their comprehension, without resorting to English.

- Putting a series of pictures in the order of the text, or vice versa, using text cut into strips.

- Comparing and perhaps contrasting text and picture.

- Jigsaw reading – one group reads a text with some of the information, the other group has a text with the rest; they then get together in pairs and reconstruct the whole story.

- Reorganising information contained in a text, e.g., reassembling a text cut into pieces, or putting a jumbled narrative into logical order.

- Drawing pictures to summarise information contained in a text.

Excerpts or independent reading?

- Completing a document.
- Mapping out or planning a document.
- Comparing several linked texts.
- Some students asking and others answering oral and written questions on a text.
- Summarising a text or, more simply, underlining or listing key words.
- Making notes, especially with a view to using the information gleaned for other purposes.

Inference and prediction exercises

- Teach students to deduce meaning from a series of statements. Which statements best fit the situation described?
- Predict the content of an article from the headline or an illustration.
- Predict what structures to expect, e.g., infinitives after modal verbs, noun/pronoun/verb positions, start and end of sub-clauses, agreeing adjectives.
- *Cloze* procedure, with words blanked out either at intervals (the shorter the interval, the harder the task) or because they are the same part of speech. You can make it easier by giving the reader a choice of possible words (perhaps with some irrelevant "distracters") or by linking it to listening. Give credit for suggestions that fit the context, even if not the original.
- A variation of *Cloze* technique: replace the blanks with non-existent words (of the appropriate part of speech), or with real words from the target language that make no sense in this context. Since students often claim that they have never seen a word before, this trains them to infer meaning from context. The task can be made easier by underlining the words to be changed, as in the boxed example below. (Note that replacing a false noun with a correct one may well change the gender.)

> Be aware that many "reading comprehension" questions can be answered without the students' having any notion of the overall meaning of the passage.

These strategies will not only help students to learn a foreign language but will also make them more aware of and interested in their own language and how it works, so the benefits will extend into many other subjects.

Par exemple . . .   *REMPLACEZ LES MOTS BIZARRES . . .*

À dix <u>secondes</u> et demie Max Moulins quitte la maison pour aller en <u>mer</u>. Dans le <u>pied</u> droit il tient son sac, dans l'autre une <u>assiette</u> – la météo a dit qu'il va pleuvoir. M. Moulins va <u>cent</u> ou trois fois en <u>mer</u>, pour faire des emplettes, pour rapporter un <u>chameau</u> à la bibliothèque, ou tout simplement pour rencontrer un <u>dragon</u>. Trois gens <u>chantent</u> déjà à l'arrêt d'<u>avion</u>, entre eux sa voisine Mme Fleuret. Il ne connaît pas les deux autres – ce sont des <u>lézards</u> assez suspects. M. Moulins parle quelques <u>mois</u> avec Mme Fleuret, et puis l'<u>avion</u> arrive. Ils sont en train de monter dans l'<u>avion</u>, quand M. Moulins entend un des <u>lézards</u> qui <u>écrit</u> à l'autre: « Ça c'est le millionnaire MM – <u>écoutes</u>-tu où il habite ? »]

Zum Beispiel . . .   *VERBESSERT DIE FALSCHEN WÖRTER . . .*

<u>Nächsten</u> Mittwoch war Evas Vater nicht zu Hause, und sie hat seinen <u>Elefant</u> genommen, um Einkäufe zu <u>verlieren</u>. Es war ein ganz <u>dünner</u> Mercedes, und sie hatte ihn nie zuvor <u>geflogen</u>. Zunächst ist alles gut gegangen – auf dem <u>Kanal</u> war wenig Verkehr, und Eva konnte ganz <u>plötzlich</u> fahren. In zehn <u>Monaten</u> hat sie den Parkplatz des <u>Supermanns</u> erreicht. Sie hat den <u>Elefant</u> in ein freies <u>Loch</u> geparkt und ist in den Laden <u>geschwommen</u>. Sie ist zunächst zur Getränkebücherei gegangen, um Rot<u>bier</u> zu suchen. Eine halbe <u>Sekunde</u> später war sie endlich fertig. Sie ist auf den Parkplatz gegangen, um den <u>Elefant</u> zu holen – er war nicht da! Verschwunden! Voller <u>Freude</u> ist sie mit dem <u>Kamel</u> nach Hause gefahren – da stand der <u>Elefant</u> vor dem Haus! Und ihr Vater <u>schlief</u> auch da! "Erstaunlich!", hat er gesagt. "Ich bin zum <u>Supermann</u> gegangen – da stand mein <u>Elefant</u> auf dem Parkplatz! Zum Glück hatte ich meinen Auto<u>schüssel</u> bei mir und konnte ihn zurück<u>tragen</u>. Ein Autodieb muss ihn wohl <u>gewaschen</u> haben."

Por ejemplo . . .   *RECTIFICA LAS PALABRAS EXTRAÑAS . . .*

Los Gómez eran dueños de una pequeña posada en el medio del bosque. No <u>comían</u> mucho dinero, así que casi <u>siempre</u> iban de vacaciones. Pero un <u>mediodía</u> ganaron un concurso en el <u>libro</u> local para una "Excursión Misteriosa". Estaban naturalmente muy <u>tristes</u>. Pidieron a una <u>enemiga</u> que se ocupe de la posada, se <u>quitaron</u> la mejor ropa, y fueron en <u>barco</u> a la ciudad. A eso de treinta <u>monos</u> esperaban a la parada de autobús. Los jóvenes <u>gateaban</u> gritando de todos partes, sus <u>nietos</u> estaban sentados alrededor <u>llorando</u> de política y del precio de los comestibles. Por fin la conductora llegó. La gente se <u>bajó del</u> bus, y la conductora les explicó que <u>oirían</u> múltiples vistas maravillosas, urbanas y rurales, y que cenarían en un sitio <u>poco</u> encantador. Se pusieron en camino, y efectivamente <u>oyeron</u> muchas <u>perros</u> interesantes, pero la <u>luna</u> estaba muy fuerte, hacía mucho <u>frío</u>, y dentro de poco los Gómez se durmieron. Cuando se despertaron, el bus se había <u>esfumado</u> y la conductora dijo:

— Hemos llegado, mis <u>enemigos</u>. ¡Encantador¡ ¿No? —

Los Gómez miraron por el <u>techo</u> – ¡el "sitio encantador" era su propia posada!

Independent reading

The National Curriculum places greatly increased emphasis on reading as an independent activity in modern foreign languages. AT3 says already at Level 3: "They are beginning to read independently . . .". Despite this, independent reading remains the Cinderella of modern languages study, yet abler students in particular can learn a lot from their own reading that they have never been taught. The rest of this chapter offers ideas on how to rescue independent reading from its present neglect.

Setting it up

- A structured reading scheme should be set up, providing books and other materials at all levels. Especially in the older year-groups, books should be supplemented by appropriate youth magazines, which have the advantage that the contents are constantly updated and are aimed at young people. Back copies can be used as source materials for all sorts of activities.

- Students should be given the necessary incentives and support, including reserved time, ready access to dictionaries and some type of reading diary.

- Students should use a graduated system of responses to books they read, from lists of emoticons or very simple multiple-choice reactions, through writing a few sentences, to longer critiques.

- Students should have opportunities to use some initiative, for example:

  ○ planning their own reading
  ○ preparing questions for other students or classes
  ○ making short presentations on what they have read.

- Systematic methods should be developed for learning vocabulary, especially phrases, whether given by you, acquired through preparing for pair- or group-work, or collected from reading (see Chapter 15). This should include the language needed to talk about books – excellent preparation for later study.

The library awareness session

A library awareness session early in the school year well repays the time spent. The school librarian can be asked to remind the students where to find each kind of book, how to use the catalogues, etc. If the library awareness session is linked to a dictionary skills exercise, this can be doubly useful (see Chapter 18). Students can be encouraged to make up reading activities for other students, including younger years.

A *"bookworm"* (*rat de bibliothèque*) booklet, written by the MFL department, can show the students what books are available. A booklet developed by one of the authors and used at an upper school in Suffolk took the form of an A5 booklet. On the front cover it had a cartoon version of a rat reading (the art department ran a competition to draw the most interesting cartoon), and separate sheets for each book or magazine read. On each sheet, students were encouraged to make a rapid assessment of their reaction to the book they had read, using smiley emoticons to indicate their degree of enjoyment. The sheet then had space for more personalised and developed criticism of the book, which could be in any language the student chose. Although the booklet was personal to the student, the teacher could ask to see it, so as to make suggestions for further reading.

It may appear strange that reading – in the normal adult sense of "independent reading" – has received so little attention in the teaching and learning of languages, despite the prominence it is given in the National Curriculum. Two factors have worked against it. First, it is not examined – enough said! Secondly, few teachers allot it a firm slot in the timetable, say, one lesson a fortnight. This is understandable, given worries about lack of time, but where it has been done, teachers have found that it was time well spent – students learnt things they were never formally taught. If you can find a way to make such an arrangement, you may well find the same.

CHAPTER 16

Using stories in the classroom

A neglected art. Reading and writing stories provides useful extension work for the more able, but can also be adapted for less able linguists – indeed, many of the activities suggested below are self-differentiating. You act as "conductor", putting questions to prompt the next step, making suggestions if the students get stuck. Most stories invite the use of ICT for word-processing, illustration, etc. If stories are written in groups, the corrected versions can be displayed or passed round and read by class-mates or other classes.

Using existing stories

Pre-narration

When introducing any narrative text, read it through before the lesson, then just tell the story from your memory, building it up by any suitable means: using pictures, getting students to suggest details, to re-narrate within groups, to produce a written group version, etc. When students then read the original text, they can identify details that differ from their own version.

Rebuilding a story

The story is heard or read, if necessary in sections, as often as needed, before being reconstructed. Especially with younger students, well-known folk tales such as *La belle et la bête* are very suitable for practising this art. Older students can provide the story, which may be taken from a recent event or family history.

Continuing a given story

Students study the first part of a story and continue it, perhaps in a given style.

Parallel stories

Having studied a story, students write one on a similar topic. This allows them to transfer the vocabulary and structures they have learnt.

Creating a story

Building a narrative

- A story is built up orally through pictures.
- Finally, in groups or the whole class, the students reconstruct the story using only the visual stimulus.
- Alternatively, it can be built up from a minimal prompt (an object or a title) by the class as a whole or by groups. If the former, the story is reconstructed or adapted in groups. If the latter, the different versions produced can be narrated to the whole class at the end. (See boxed example below.)

Inventing a story in class

This can make a very productive session, involving the whole class or groups as appropriate.

i.   A title is given or agreed. It can be linked to the current topic, but slightly quirky subjects work best – *"a day in the life of a house-mouse"*, *"an invisible (wo)man goes shopping"*, *"a train journey with a pet snake"* . . .

ii. The general plan is worked out from students' suggestions, written up, displayed and noted down by the students. The details are filled in step by step and noted down, in a whole-class activity. Alternatively, groups of four to six students could each be asked to take on one part of the story, which would mean that the story would come together as a whole, or each group could be asked to write their version of the story, resulting in as many stories as there are groups in the classroom.

iii. If this is done as a whole-class activity, with the bare details being displayed, a final activity could be a class narration of the story. If the small groups each construct one part of the story, then each separate group could relate their part, to approval or discussion by the others. If each group constructs its own story, then this can become a class vote for the best story. Whichever final outcome is chosen, we have a collaborative project happening in class, with lots of opportunity for peer- and self-assessment, for suggestions for improvement, for scaffolding and for reformulation – all plus points for acquisition.

Linking unrelated pictures

Given unrelated pictures of (1) a person or persons, (2) an object and (3) a place or event, students invent a story to link the three. This again could be a small-group collaborative task.

Using stories in the classroom

Story consequences

Give each pair a sheet of paper with the first sentence of a story at the top. They add a sentence and pass the sheet (unfolded) to the next pair. This continues round the class/group until the last pair, who must write a conclusion. This will need careful orchestration by you – with each change of person, you state what the next stage will be. Example for a story involving a chance meeting of two old friends: First change = "Where are they?". Second change = "Who else is there?". Third change = "What are they wearing?", and so on.

Imagining a scene from a visual source

Given an image, students imagine what must have happened beforehand, is happening now, may happen next. Collect a file of suitably ambiguous and interesting pictures. (See also picture in Chapter 14.)

Imagining a scene from a heard source

Eyes closed, the students focus on a recorded series of sounds and the images they evoke. The outcome can range from single words to short paragraphs, produced by the whole class, groups, pairs or individuals. (See also Chapter 13, "Focus on the music".)

Par exemple . . .   *HISTOIRES IMAGINÉES . . .*

Prof: Bonjour, tout le monde. Aujourd'hui j'ai apporté quelque chose d'intéressant. Qu'est-ce que c'est ?

Luke: Un bucket, Madame ?

Prof: Très drôle ! En français peut-être ? Cherchez-le dans vos dictionnaires.

Mia: C'est un seau, Madame.

Prof: Exacte ! Qu'est-ce qu'il y a dans le seau ?

Ethan: Rien, Madame.

Prof: Exacte ! Maintenant, formez vos groupes et imaginez l'histoire de ce seau. S'il vous faut un mot, cherchez-le dans vos dicos ou demandez-le-moi !

Groupe I	*Groupe II*	*Groupe III*
Dylan: Je crois que ce seau appartenait à une jeune fille – ou à son papa . . .	*Jade*: Selon moi, ce seau a servi à cueillir quelque chose, des fruits ou des légumes, par exemple.	*Noah*: Avez-vous remarqué ces deux trous dans le seau ?

Chloe: ...et elle voulait tester l'eau de la rivière qui coulait dans les prés derrière sa maison...

Lucy: ...parce que son prof de bio a demandé à la classe de faire un projet environnemental.

Dylan: Donc, elle a pris ce seau (sans demander la permission du papa), et elle est allée à la rivière chercher de l'eau.

Poppy: Mais les rives de la rivière étaient très glissantes et...

Lucy: ...elle est tombée dans l'eau !

Oliver: Heureusement, elle savait nager et elle a réussi à se hisser hors de la rivière.

Poppy: Elle était trempée jusqu'aux os, mais elle avait un seau plein d'eau !

Chloe: Malheureusement, elle n'avait pas remarqué que le seau avait deux petits trous...

Oliver: ...et en arrivant à la maison elle avait beaucoup d'eau dans ses vêtements mais rien dans le seau !

Luke: Peut-être, mais quoi ? Et pourquoi ?

Ethan: Quelque chose de peu licite, ça c'est certain !

Maisie: Peut-être que deux ados l'ont trouvé et ils l'ont utilisé pour chiper des pommes dans le verger de leur voisin.

Jade: Alors, ils sont entrés dans le verger en passant par un trou dans la haie et...

Max: ...ils ont trouvé un bel arbre où il y avait des tas de pommes par terre sous l'arbre.

Maisie: Mais beaucoup de ces pommes n'étaient pas vraiment mangeables...

Max: ...tandis que les pommes qui étaient toujours sur l'arbre étaient superbes!

Ethan: Ils commençaient à cueillir des pommes quand...

Luke: ...le voisin est arrivé – et il n'était pas du tout content !

Jade: Les ados se sont sauvés à toute vitesse, mais toutes les pommes sont tombées par terre et...

Maisie: ...il ne leur est resté que le seau vide !

Ruby: Oui, ça lui donnait presque l'air d'un casque!

Harry: D'accord – et je crois que c'est parce que quelqu'un l'a utilisé comme casque.

Jacob: Comment?

Emily: Ah! Je comprends ! Un jeune étudiant a appris par Twitter qu'on allait organiser une grande manifestation contre la hausse envisagée des frais universitaires.

Ruby: Il voulait participer, mais sa famille ne devrait pas le savoir...

Harry: ...parce qu'ils n'approuvaient pas 'cette espèce de bagarre délinquante', et il ne voulait pas perdre l'argent qu'ils lui donnaient ?

Evie: Exacte ! Donc, pour pouvoir voir, il a percé ces deux trous dans le seau et...

Ethan: ...il est allé à la manifestation déguisé en chevalier errant !

Ruby: Il était très fier de son casque, il criait comme un fou, mais ...

Evie: ...soudain la police est arrivée, tout le monde s'est sauvé, et son casque est resté dans les mains de la police !

> **Prof:** OK, ça suffit ! Vous avez bien travaillé. Maintenant, chaque groupe choisit un narrateur qui va nous conter l'histoire de son groupe. Allez-y !

The very idea of using a story invites creativity, a skill that is often neglected. In a small group, it becomes a collaborative creativity. The activities described above use different stimuli, with different outcomes. One such outcome could be an improvisation competition between different classes in a year group, or between schools, and then even extending to partner schools in another country.[1] Listing different ways of using stories is only limited ... by our imagination!

---

[1] A variation of this idea, an inter-university debate competition, was presented by Denis Guezais and Pierre Laurent at the RANACLES (Rassemblement des Centres de Langues) conference in Nice in 2008.

CHAPTER 17

Making good use of written work

(See also many examples in Chapter 9.)

Written work is sometimes regarded as an entity, separate from other linguistic skills. It can also be seen as inherently more "difficult" than speaking or listening. While this is certainly true for students who have always struggled to read and write, it is the reverse for many others, not least because the process of writing has the great advantage that it allows time for reflection, change of mind, correction. In fact, writing, *per se*, is neither easier nor harder than speaking, it is simply a complementary skill that, properly used, can be of great benefit, especially in fixing acquired language in a student's mind. Many of the activities already described demonstrate this, and this should be borne in mind as we now look more specifically at various aspects of the skill of writing.

The purposes of students' writing

Reasons for students' writing in the target language include:

- as an aid to memory, creating a "language store" (see Chapter 19)
- as a check on spelling
- as a means of communication: short messages, emails, (replies to) postcards and letters, recounting events, etc.
- for language games, such as "to-and-fro dialogues", "chain sentences" or "consequences" (see Chapter 9)
- to challenge others: puzzles, quizzes . . .
- to record and store information, from short memo notes upwards
- as a means of self-expression through stories, opinions, jokes, poems . . .

Readership

Not surprisingly, most written work in schools is done for the teacher, and to some extent this will always be true. But there are many other possibilities. Working outwards from the student, other intended readers can include:

- the student herself/himself, mainly making rough notes and recording vocabulary and structures for (re-)learning (see Chapter 19)
- the student's immediate partner(s) in pair- or group-work (see Chapters 8 and 9)
- the rest of the class, especially through display
- wider circulation, to other classes and years, for newsletters, for sending (by email or post) to foreign partner schools.

The choice of intended reader has a significant influence of the balance between conveying a message and grammatical correctness. Generally speaking, the wider the readership, the more important it is to avoid errors of form or syntax. We discuss this much-debated subject below.

Types of writing

A language learner is likely to encounter three main types of writing, each with its own grammatical and lexical emphasis. If you are aware of this, it makes it much easier to link writing to the structures and vocabulary the class is currently studying. If you adopt a full-scale task-based approach to language learning, then the written task itself can be the pretext for a focus on form, either as a "time out" during the writing process or once the task is completed. In the former, you may see that a particular structure is blocking the writing, in which case a "time out" is necessary in order to clarify the structure. In the latter, the need for clarification may be apparent during the writing process but the students may be getting round the problem, so it can be left until the end.

Descriptive writing

- A preponderance of nouns over verbs.
- Tenses/aspects (especially past tenses) associated with ongoing features rather than one-off action.
- Adjectives, their agreement and endings.
- Prepositions and conjunctions of place.
- Natural topics: My home/school/town, the countryside, the way XXX is/was organised, . . .

Narrative writing

- A preponderance of verbs over nouns.
- Tenses/aspects (especially past tenses) concerned both with taking the action forward and with setting the scene or background.
- Adverbs, their construction and positioning.
- Prepositions and conjunctions of time and manner.
- Natural topics: A family/class/school trip, a historical event, a report on an accident/burglary/mugging . . .

Expository writing (explanation/argument – more advanced)

- More abstract nouns.
- Greater use of conditional tenses, perhaps imperatives, modals.
- Increased use of subordinate clauses.
- Natural topics: For/against school uniform/compulsory military service/equal rights for XXX . . .

Imaginative writing

Creative writing may have elements of any of the types discussed above, or (especially in the case of poetry) none of them. It need not be thought of as more difficult than more prosaic forms of writing – indeed, poetry can be the simplest type of writing: we have seen very effective poems consisting simply of nouns. In addition, the level of difficulty can be adjusted by the support given.

Many of the following activities are suitable as group activities with joint or individual written results. They can also lead to brief presentations to the class or a group. Depending on the ability level of the class, they could include:

- composing brochures for local attractions or imaginary products
- composing stories, sketches or poems, and perhaps "publishing" these for other students to enjoy
- writing instructions for other students to follow – good practice in use of *one does* . . . . (see boxed example below)
- constructing quizzes to be answered by partners or other classes or years
- adapting texts into a different format; for example, dramatising a prose passage or, conversely, preparing a journalistic or police report on an event seen on video

Making good use of written work

- recounting family, local or national events
- writing or making notes about their own recent experiences, hobbies or interests
- conducting and writing up simple surveys either within the class or more broadly within the school or beyond it
- imagining the story line of a popular target culture soap opera – write about what happened to key characters yesterday, what they are doing in today's episode or tomorrow
- writing an SMS or Twitter poem in the target language, with all the constraints of text messaging, and make this a competition, with a prize for the best poem
- students from the exchange school write a piece in English, students in the British school write in the target language, and a class book is produced.

Par exemple . . .	COMMENT . . .	
. . . faire du café.	. . . faire un sandwich au fromage.	. . . faire un lit.
. . . entretenir un vélo.	. . . préparer un pique-nique.	. . . acheter un ordinateur.
. . . acheter un billet.	. . . réserver une chambre.	. . . laver une voiture.

Zum Beispiel . . .	WIE . . .	
. . . kocht man Kaffee?	. . . macht man ein Käsebrot?	. . . macht man ein Bett?
. . . pflegt man einen Rasenmäher?	. . . deckt man den Tisch?	. . . kauft man Schuhe?
. . . kauft man eine Fahrkarte?	. . . bucht man ein Hotelzimmer?	. . . wäscht man ein Auto?

Por ejemplo . . .	¿CÓMO SE . . .	
. . . abre una botella de vino?	. . . compran aspirinas?	. . . pone la mesa?
. . . mantiene une bicicleta?	. . . limpian zapatos?	. . . reserva un cuarto de hotel?
. . . hace una cama?	. . . hace un café con leche?	. . . vende un ordenador?

Communicating meaning vs. correct language

This age-old dispute rests on a false dichotomy, in that even minor misuse of a structure or syntax can easily distort meaning. (In English, for example, "She spoke sharply to the girls who weren't listening" has a quite different meaning from "She spoke sharply to the girls, who weren't listening".) This is especially true of writing, where the reader often can't ask the writer to clear up misunderstandings. In L2 learning, therefore, any strategies that improve grammatical accuracy are to be welcomed, but the crucial questions are: How much does correcting every error contribute to this aim? May it even impede students' progress?

As so often, the answer to these questions depends largely on context. The more advanced the student, the fewer will be the errors arising from ignorance rather than carelessness, but the more desirable it is to single out the former and correct them. In the earlier years, however, and (ironically) particularly when students are encouraged to use their initiative and try out new forms of writing, to see one's work spattered with red is very discouraging. Various ways out of this quandary suggest themselves, as follows.

- Using small groups, have each student read and correct another's work, preferably in pencil. This has several advantages:

  ○ knowing that one of their partners is going to read their work has a noticeable effect on students' efforts to write correctly

  ○ the partner's pencilled corrections are much less daunting than a teacher's red ink – and they can be challenged

  ○ you are given an insight not only into the original writers' accuracy but also into their partners'.

- Especially when a certain structure has just been practised, or when irritating basic errors predominate, reach an agreement with students that errors in that structure will be strongly marked down. You can then decide which other errors can stand and which need to be corrected.

- In conjunction with this, home in on an error that students' work has shown to be prevalent in the class and mount a concerted attack on it. Get students to create displays that demonstrate the correct usage.

- An important principle to get across to the learner is that error is normal. It is part of the construction of a new language. All learners construct an interlanguage, intermediate between the two languages, and it is within this interlanguage that they try out new forms, new structures. While they are trying them out, error is an inevitable and important part of the process and shows them and you where work is needed.

Public display

Especially when the final text is to be put on display or passed to another class, it is not good practice to allow gross mistakes through, as this simply reinforces error. You can avoid this, without restricting the initial writing, by mimicking the processes of a publishing house: the draft text goes first to the "group editor" (a student), then to the "editor-in-chief" (the teacher), who judges which mistakes should be corrected (and how) before the text is "published".

This chapter has looked at a wide range of types and purposes of students' writing, from one or two words through short pieces such as instructions and notes to longer accounts of events and imaginative writing limited only by time and creativity. We hope to have shown that all students, even the least literate, can benefit by writing. The crucial thing is to be clear about its purpose and the likely demands on the writer's knowledge of structure and vocabulary and, in the case of free writing, her/his imagination. By identifying and preparing for potential pitfalls, you can make many tasks possible that might otherwise be very difficult.

CHAPTER 18

Dictionary and reference skills

Pupils should be able to . . . use reference materials such as dictionaries appropriately and effectively.[1]

Dictionaries may be books or online. The same goes for other sources of information such as encyclopaedias. However, for the language learner, the bilingual book-dictionary is in many ways the most convenient source of lexical information – many students actually prefer leafing through a book to using an electronic version. Some reputable editions are cheap, so each student can have one, which makes looking up a word much faster than online; and like all dictionaries, they offer information the searcher didn't know s/he wanted but might well find useful or interesting. A book also enables students to engage in all sorts of language-learning activities that are not possible otherwise. We therefore start by considering book-dictionaries, and later go on to other sources of information.

From as early as possible, all students should be taught how to use dictionaries. You should deliberately use one in class to show that "experts" also use this support.

- Ensure that students know where to find the dictionaries and other reference texts.

- Plan for a dictionary skills session at the beginning of every school year, and repeat later if needed. Don't neglect basic skills, such as looking in the right half of the book, using head-words properly, interpreting abbreviations.

- The alphabetic order in the target language may differ from English. Revising the alphabet can in itself be a valuable exercise for less able students. It also highlights different letters such as the Ñ in Spanish, and the

---

[1] Modern Foreign Languages Programme of Study: key stage 3 (2008) §2.1e.

fact that from 2012 Spanish CH and LL no longer have their own separate entries. (See also chapter 11, Learning an alphabet.)

Ignorance of these features can cause unexpected problems. Dictionaries may be permitted in some types of examination, so understanding correct usage is key.

Using dictionaries

Students can use dictionaries to look up a word they've have heard in conversation, and even when preparing to speak in class. But almost always dictionaries are used to search for unfamiliar words encountered in reading (TL → English) or needed when writing (English → TL).

Reading

Unless they are translating a text, students do not need to look up every unfamiliar word. They should develop the skill of picking out the key words, words essential to the meaning of the passage. This is true both when reading independently and when tackling a shorter extract as an exercise. You can help by selecting a text with a number of unfamiliar words and challenging students to identify the ones that they would need to look up; they should suggest the meanings, giving their reasons, which will be checked for accuracy at the end of the exercise. Before dictionaries are brought into play, students should also say what part of speech the various words belong to; this knowledge is crucial when looking for the correct rendering in the dictionary. For example: English *fast* – noun? verb? adjective? adverb?

Students need to recognise the dangers of using online translators to translate a full text; this can produce quite inaccurate versions. This is in contrast to the benefits of looking up individual items of vocabulary on reputable sites such as www.wordreference.com.

Writing

At any stage of their course, students are likely to need to look up words they need for their writing. They can partially circumvent this by finding ways to use their existing knowledge to express what they want to say. These "compensation strategies" are a very valuable skill. You can also minimise the use of a dictionary by asking students to say (in English) which words they think they would need to write about a given topic; gather these together and either simply translate them, using a dictionary yourself if need be, or (better) distribute the words to groups, who look them up and offer their translations. Students then take down and learn the agreed versions before writing their pieces.

Possible dictionary exercises

- A timed race through the dictionary to find a specific list of words.
- Finding the correct translation, into or out of the target language, of a word given in context.
- Looking up words with a number of different meanings, e.g., *train* (English or French) or *Zug* (German). Encourage students to tease out differences and possible connections, and get them to use each meaning in different sentences.
- Illustrating the dangers of dictionaries by selective use of "clangers" such as *je suis percé* "I'm bored", *match de box* "matchbox" or *sur le marsouin* "on purpose" (both the latter are actual students' offerings, the first showing complete neglect of context, the second showing that students can't always spell English!).
- Collecting collocations, i.e., words that naturally belong together:
  - either syntactically (*se souvenir/ . . . de, aider/ . . . à*) or
  - semantically (*un coup de main/pied/œil/fil/ . . .*).
- Finding synonyms and opposites (if possible using a thesaurus or synonym dictionary – see below) and using them in sentences.
- Meaning chains: look up any target language or English word, pick one of its translations and look that up in the other half of the dictionary, pick a *different* translation there and look that up, . . . Write a sentence for each word in the target language. If done for homework, the results can be checked by partners. (See example below, given without the sentences.)

Par exemple . . .   UN MOT MÈNE À L'AUTRE . . .

Game – *jeu* – play – *pièce* – room – *place* – square – *carré* – straight – *droit* – law – *loi* – rule – *règle* – ruler – *dirigeant* – leader – *chef* – head – *tête* . . .

Zum Beispiel . . .   EINE ZWEISPRACHIGE WORTKETTE . . .

Road – *Strasse* – straits – *Nöte* – troubles – *Unruhe* – noise – *Lärm* – row – *Krach* – crash – *Schlag* – type – *Art* – way – *Weg* – track – *Spur* – scrap – *Fetzen* – rag – *Käseblatt* . . .

Por ejemplo . . .   UNA CADENA BILINGÜE DE PALABRAS . . .

Table – *mesa* – board – *tabla* – panel – *equipo* – team – *yunta* – yoke – *canesú* – bodice – *cuerpo* – body – *cadáver* – carcass – *armazón* – frame – *marco* – goalposts – *portería* . . .

Thesauruses and synonym dictionaries

These works are available in any language students are likely to be learning (see footnote[2] for four examples). Word-processors also have appended thesauruses. Jumping around in the target language synonym dictionary gives an enjoyable sense of adventure, and can add spice to many of the activities described above. For example, students can:

- look up synonyms for an English word and note some of them down
- translate the original word into the target language, look up synonyms in a TL dictionary and note some down
- try to pair up the English and TL synonyms. How well do they match? What are the main differences?
- write a sentence for five words in each language. What does that say about the differences between them?

This exercise can teach students a lot about cultural differences between the two countries. Some languages may also turn out to have many more synonyms than others, which is an indication of each side's breadth of vocabulary. Students may discover that there is probably no such thing as a genuine synonym.

For example . . .	*SYNONYMS IN FOUR LANGUAGES . . .*
thief *Synonyms (16 out of 92):* bandit, booster, burglar, cracksman, cutpurse, dacoit, dip, filcher, footpad, nip, pilferer, prig, robber, ruffian, scofflaw, thug	**voleur** *Synonymes (16 de 27):* aigrefin, bandit, brigand, cambrioleur, escroc, filou, fraudeur, fripon, gangster, larron, malfaiteur, pickpocket, pillard, pirate, resquilleur, truand
Dieb *Synonyme (16 aus 62):* Bandit, Betrüger, Ganove, Krimineller, Raüber, Schurke, Verbrecher, Erpresser, Gewalttäter, Hehler, Schieber, Schuft, Spitzbube, Schwindler, Strolch, Gangster	**ladrón** *Sinónimos (16 de 37):* carterista, caco, ratero, cleptómano, descuidero, chorizo, mangante, saqueador, timador, bandido, atracador, maleante, cuatrero, bajamano, rufián, baile

---

[2] www.synonymes.com, http://synonyme.woxikon.de, www.diccionariodesinonimos.es, http://dizionari.corriere.it/dizionario_sinonimi_contrari/M/momentaneo.shtml

Encyclopaedias

Encyclopaedias, printed or online, can provide students with valuable information for their topic, including some that they may not have been looking for. Students of foreign languages need access to encyclopaedias in the target language. In book form this includes works such as *Le Petit Larousse, Der Volks-Brockhaus, Pequeño Larousse Ilustrado*. Online, the immense range of offerings can be very confusing, especially as many of those listed as search results are highly specialised. The best resource for language learners is probably the well-known Wikipedia.[3] Its "List of Wikipedias" (see footnote[3]) shows selected languages at the top of the page; these lead to an article about the language in question. Lower down are listed the 283 languages for which it has articles; clicking on the name in the *Language (local)* column brings up the complete site in that language. From here students can search for a relevant article, using appropriate key words until they are satisfied.

Why, though, should language learners want to consult an encyclopaedia? Students of fact-based subjects will be looking for information. Language learners can discover much about the culture of the country in question, but it will be at least as important to them to broaden their grasp of the target language. For this reason, any text they retrieve can be treated in the same way as a paper-based text, as described in Chapter 14, but:

1 students are searching for information that has value for them, not just as a linguistic exercise

2 such texts are more ephemeral, normally studied online, not printed out.

Once students have found a relevant article, a suitable approach is as follows.

- They study the text either by themselves or (better) with a partner.
- Working separately, each makes a list of 10 or so key words.
- They write a sentence that summarises the import of the text, or just a suitable headline.
- They compare their key words and sentence with their partner's, supporting their selection with reference to the on-screen text.
- Without reference to the screen, they write an "abstract" of the text.
- They bring the text back up and compare it with their abstract. What have they added? What omitted?
- They underline any information in their abstract that was new to them and use it in the activity on which the online search was based. What have they learnt about the culture of the country in question?

---

[3] http://meta.wikimedia.org/wiki/List_of_Wikipedias

Dictionary and reference skills

With dictionaries and other reference works the same principle applies as in many areas of human activity: practice makes, if not perfect, at least competent. Competence develops as students get used to consulting reference works without wasting time (a common criticism of dictionaries), but also without missing opportunities to expand their knowledge in previously unforeseen directions. As they refine their "reference skills", they'll find that dictionaries, and especially encyclopaedias, are not just necessary tools but also a genuine source of interest and enjoyment. This is an important step on the route to becoming a competent linguist.

CHAPTER 19

Learning words and phrases

Students should be able to ... develop techniques for memorising words, phrases and spellings.[1]

Knowledge of words and phrases is the very stuff of language, without which communication is impossible. One of the most common complaints of language learners is that they lack vocabulary, but few of them know where to begin to learn it. Activities described throughout this book depend crucially on students' having sufficient grasp both of general ("core") language and of lexis specific to the current topic. Core language in particular must be regularly refreshed throughout the years of the course – which raises the question "How?". Most of the responsibility naturally falls on the students themselves, and these notes suggest some ways in which they can gather, learn and retain words, phrases and short extracts.

Helping students to learn

You can help the process along in various ways, for example the following.

- It is vital to pay attention to ways in which students retrieve a lexical item after it has been learnt. Comprehension problems, especially in listening, are often caused by non-recognition of an item. This is one of the reasons why it is so important to introduce a new item phonologically before the written form. And to include it in any personal dictionary that students make for themselves (see Chapter 10 on the co-construction of a glossary using ICT).

- Another potentially important skill is to recognise the link between the sound and how it is written. How many different ways are there of spelling the phoneme /ō/, for example? (See Chapter 6, "Training the ear".)

---

[1] Modern Foreign Languages Programme of Study: key stage 3 (2008) §2.1b.

Learning words and phrases

- High-frequency words make up 80–90% of a text, so it makes sense to start by learning these and then to introduce lower-frequency words to supplement these essential words. (The link in footnote[2] leads to lists of high-frequency words in any language students are likely to be learning.)

- It is often useful to devote a session to strategies for learning and retaining words and phrases. This approach has been used successfully by one of the authors with various publics.

- Certain topics will of their nature involve particular structures; you can reinforce this on the spot by a brisk revision of other related structures.

- Especially when your assessments have revealed certain weaknesses, take a few minutes at the start or end of a lesson to swiftly revise them. This is a time when flash-cards are very useful; they can be pictorial, but they can also display phrases with the relevant language missing, to be supplied either in a plenary session, or within groups (see below, "Visual support").

- Partners can set each other tests, perhaps from each other's vocab book. If they use word-cards (see below, "Techniques for memorising . . ."), these can be used in a memory game.

- Don't forget that the students themselves can produce this type of resource; quite apart from the labour this saves you, it is important to reinforce their feeling of ownership of the course – and they may well be more skilled at it than you are!

The nature of the language to be learnt

Retrieval of a word is stimulated by creative work. Techniques for learning vocabulary provide a clear example of the main tenet of this book – *learning by doing* – using the vocabulary will help you to learn it. Interestingly, research has shown that words learnt through discussing their meaning are more likely to be retained (75%) than those learnt without discussion (57%) (Newton, 1995 – see "Further reading"), and observing the discussion is as useful as being involved in it! When students learn vocabulary they need to move it from short-term to long-term memory, and rehearsing the word, rolling it around in the mind, playing with it, taking risks as they try to use it, are all good techniques for facilitating this. Other points of interest are as follows.

- *Un mot n'est rien sans sa phrase* (said by a teacher from West Africa). A phrase is much easier to learn and retain than individual words learnt separately.

---

[2] http://en.wiktionary.org/wiki/Wiktionary:Frequency_lists

- Similarly, a series of phrases is easier to learn and retain if it has a common context – normally the current topic.

- Especially in the early stages, nouns and adjectives tend to dominate – more attention needs to be given to other parts of speech, especially verbs, prepositions/postpositions and linking words.

- Emphasise core language, i.e., non-topic-specific phrases and structures (see Chapter 5) and insist on students using it, especially when they write.

- It is especially important to learn and *use* the vocabulary of questions.

The composition of the word itself can affect learning and retrieval. For example:

- *morphological transparency*: a compound word is easier to learn if each of its component parts has meaning, e.g. *hope, hopeful, hopeless*

- *derivational complexity*: it is/is not clear how the word was put together, e.g. *child, childless, childlessness*

- *inflexional regularity*: the different cases, tenses, aspects, etc. are/are not regular, e.g., plurals *hat, hats* vs. *child, children*, or tense/aspect formation such as *listen, listened, listened* vs. *bring, brought, brought* or *go, went, gone*

- *sound–script consistency*: the word is/is not pronounced as it is spelt, e.g. no traps *cot, dot, hot, lot, not* vs. traps e.g., *rough, cough, plough, through, though*, etc.

- interestingly, *word-length* has no clear effect on learnability; indeed, young children learning to read may well find *aeroplane* easier to recognise than *then* or *there*.

Ownership

Retention doubles if a word or phrase is first encountered in a meaningful way. If students have to make an effort in order to make sense of the new word or structure, then they begin to own the word and to make it part of their vocabulary. A feeling of "ownership" is a very important aspect of students' attitude to their work. This is a universal feeling – we all know how encouraging it is to feel "I had a part in this!" – but it applies especially to our present subject. Students are much more likely both to learn words, phrases and structures and to remember them if they feel some responsibility for choosing them. Clearly, this is possible only to a limited extent, but the feeling should be encouraged.

- An orderly vocabulary notebook or file (a "personal dictionary") is a first essential. It enables students not only to record words and phrases you give them but also to build up their own "language store" from other sources (especially their reading).

- Get students to list in English the words and phrases they feel they would need for a given task (this can be done for homework). In class, either gather these in and use them to help you prepare a list in the target language or (better) ask for suggestions, write up the target language equivalents and have students copy, learn and use them.

- Instead of dictating the vocabulary to be learnt, ask students to arrive each week at a given time with a list in English, on the left of a sheet of paper, of 10 to 20 words, phrases and sentences they claim to have learnt in the previous week (you will soon spot the ones whose lists are always the same). Give them a few minutes to write in the answers, then take the sheets in and mark them yourself – experience has shown that, because the list has been chosen by the students, the answers are almost always much more correct (and therefore much quicker to mark) than those on an imposed list. Give plus points for really good entries – students can then get more than 100%!

- Instead of bringing in a list in English, more able students especially can bring in a list of synonyms or definitions of the learnt items, or vice versa. (This is normal in English as Additional Language (EAL) classes.)

Techniques for memorising words, phrases and spellings

The classic sequence for vocabulary (and grammar and syntax) is *notice–comprehend–acquire*. The student notices a new word, structure, syntax, etc., tries to make sense of it, and learns it. However, the learning stage is often a rather haphazard affair, where the student stares at a list, repeats it *x* times and hopes it sticks. To introduce some system into learning, here are three possible techniques among many. They all work well, though the third requires some organisation. All vocabulary learning requires commitment, perseverance and frequent opportunities to use what one has learnt. But it's well worth it!

Look–cover–write–check

This is the simplest technique, used both in MFL and English departments and in teaching literacy. The student:

- looks at the English word(s) and the target language equivalent
- covers one or the other
- writes down the hidden word(s)
- removes the cover and checks for accuracy.

Down–up–down learning

In this technique, the student:

- takes a list of about 10 words or phrases (half a side in a vocabulary notebook is ideal)
- covers either the English (easier) or the target language (harder) and, starting at the top, "tests" the first word
- after two seconds, uncovers the answer and goes on to the next entry
- on reaching the bottom, immediately goes back up in the same fashion, but in the reverse order
- continues down and up like this until s/he can do three runs without a mistake
- checks by testing at random in the list
- re-tests at intervals to refresh the memory.

Word cards

This is a method reportedly developed by the US navy to help sailors learn signal flags, where there is seldom any relation between the image and its message. Here the student:

- takes a box (e.g., a shoe-box) and puts in eight dividers marked *Day 1* to *Day 4* and *Week 1* to *Week 4, or* (simpler) labels eight envelopes *Day 1* to *Day 4* and *Week 1* to *Week 4*
- collects material from reading, course book, class lessons, etc.
- writes English words or (better) short phrases on one side of small cards or slips of paper and the target language on the other; each new card goes into *Day 1*
- each Monday, Tuesday, Wednesday and Thursday, "tests" all the cards in *Days 1 to 4, starting with Day 4*, allowing only two seconds to respond. If a card "passes", it is promoted to the next *Day*; if it "fails", it goes back to *Day 1*. (*Day 4* passes go to *Week 1*.) Giving the English from the target language is naturally easier than vice versa
- on *Friday*, tests all the *Week* cards, *starting with Week 4*. "Passes" are promoted to the next *Week*, "failures" go *right back to Day 1*. Once a card has passed *Week 4* it counts as learnt – though it still needs to be used.

Memorising short extracts

Like story-telling (see Chapter 16), this is a valuable though little-used art, well worth practising. Even beginners can learn brief couplets, jokes, Q & A, etc., which both train the memory and increase their stock of idioms. If they compose these themselves, they have great opportunities for inventiveness. They can progress to learning short authentic extracts, especially poems. It can be quite surprising to see the enjoyment and sense of achievement this gives even students of whom you would never have thought it.

Visual support

The association of a word with an image is essential for many students, in particular the less able. Make up flashcards/photobanks/wall-charts/realia/OHTs to support the course – *or better still, get students to do it.* (See also Chapter 6.)

Good uses of flashcards include:

- frequent repetition of the word accompanied by the flashcard or object, leading to
- the flashcard/object used to elicit the word, leading to
- guessing what card you (or group members) are holding
- matching flashcard to the spoken word
- matching flashcard to the written word.

Some of these can be team games within a class, or group activities. For verbs denoting action, visual support can also be given by a mimed action or gesture.

A form of visual support that can be very helpful in languages with non-Roman script is "air-drawing". Here, students have to learn not only the new lexis and structures but also the script. To take Chinese, you can demonstrate by "drawing" the constituent parts of an ideograph, building up to the complete sign. Pairs of students then take it in turns to "draw" the sign in the air; their partner guesses what it is, and they then practise writing it on paper. The same can be done, for example, with the letters or words of Russian, Arabic/Urdu, Hindi or Japanese *kana*.

Linked meanings: Word-association and word-formation

- Many students learn vocabulary through association. Encourage them to look for synonyms and antonyms. Similarly, phrases are often more easily remembered as a whole than their constituent parts separately. Get students to record vocabulary in phrases, or with related words.

- Get students to deduce the meanings of words from known related words, for example, *ménage/emménager/déménager/ménagère*. They can search for corresponding nouns, verbs, adjectives, adverbs and so on, and link them in a diagram (see boxed example below).

- Show students how the target language links words together to express more complex ideas; for example, nouns are mainly linked by prepositions in Romance languages, but joined to make compounds in Germanic languages (including noun-strings in English).

- Especially in Germanic and Slavonic languages, prefixes play a very important role. Students can write sentences using the same prefix with different verbs, or vice versa, and ask themselves what the meaning of each prefix is.

Zum Beispiel...   *WAS SAGT DIESES PRÄFIX?...*

ich **ent**komme, **ent**fliehe, **ent**ziffere es, **ent**schuldige mich, **ent**binde ihn, **ent**ferne es...

- Make students aware of the sound/spelling links between languages, for example:
  - English *th/d/t/p/gh* ↔ German *d/t/(t)z/(p)f/ch* respectively;
  - English *st-* ↔ French *ét-* ↔ Spanish *est-*;
  - English/French *f/pl* ↔ Spanish *h/ll* (+ Italian *pi*) respectively.

Students can compete to collect linked pairs of words and use them in sentences.

Diagrams

These include the following.

- The *tree*, with the central word at the top, divided downwards into smaller and smaller branches. For example, house contents can be classified in tree form with the different rooms in the house forming the main branches, the main items the smaller branches, and the smaller items the smallest branches/leaves.
- *Folders.* In ICT files are grouped in folders; do the same with lexical items.
- *Mind maps* and *concept maps*. See Chapter 20, "Examples of exercises" (thinking skills).

Use of definitions

Definitions can help students to identify and understand key words in a text. This can be extended to cover any words or phrases, as follows.

1 Print the vocabulary on one set of slips of paper, and the definitions on another.

2 Distribute the vocabulary to one half of the class and the definitions to the other.

3 The words/phrases and their definitions are matched ... *either* by students moving around until they find their opposite number *or* (best in groups) by a

student calling out a definition and another responding with the matching vocabulary (or vice versa).

4 If sufficient copies are produced (preferably by students), the two sets of slips can be used as the basis for a memory game (Pelmanism) in groups of three or four:

  i.   the slips are laid face down on the desk
  ii. players take turns to pick up slips, trying to match words and definitions
  iii. a player who matches word with definition retains the slips and has another go
  iv. if the slips do not match, both are put back on the desk, face down, and the next player has a go
  v.   the game continues until no slips are left on the desk.

With able students such activities can lead to using monolingual dictionaries, including on the Web.

Similar techniques include:

● Finishing a sentence for someone, e.g.:

A *On est allé . . .* B *A Rome ? A Paris ? Au marché ?*
A *Non, au café. Et on a commandé . . .* B *Un coca ? Une bière ? Un café ?*
A *Non, un sandwich au . . . etc.*

● Searching for words by defining them – teach the words for "thing", "to use", etc.:

A *C'est un truc qu'on utilise pour écrire.*
B *Ah, tu veux dire un stylo/un bic/un crayon/une machine à écrire.*

● Conversely, B gives a definition of a word provided by A.

A *Un stylo/un bic, qu'est-ce que c'est ?*
B *C'est un truc qu'on utilise pour écrire.*

● Students look for groups of words denoting a gradation of meaning, e.g:

jamais → *rarement* → *quelquefois* → *souvent* → *toujours*
glacial → *froid* → *frais* → *tiède* → *chaud* → *bouillant*

To repeat the first sentence of this chapter: "Knowledge of words and phrases is the very stuff of language, without which communication is impossible." However, even in one's mother tongue, if this knowledge is never used, it soon fades – we all know how a word can be "on the tip of my tongue", unavailable for use. For this reason, while we hope that our various suggestions will help students to learn the words and phrases of the target language, the more their work is planned to recycle previous experience, the more likely is it that this knowledge will stick.

Integrating grammar into communication

Mieux vaut une tête bien faite qu'une tête bien pleine.

(Montaigne)

The role of grammar in language learning

There are two clearly distinguishable views of the place of grammar. One is that the student should start with an understanding of the language structure, before using it in closely prescribed exercises and then in freer performance. In this case the primary focus is on form or forms, with meaning coming afterwards. Learning is seen as incremental, with a clear progression to the introduction of each structure.

Unfortunately, life isn't like that: a novice may well need to talk of past or future events; a young learner of French exposed to stories written for primary school children will encounter the *passé simple*; and so on. There is no doubt that explicit learning of grammar results in successful short-term learning, for a grammar test, for example. But students find it difficult to use that knowledge in a communicative task. They will need frequent reminders in order to use it.

The other view sees grammar as arising out of performance, with a primary focus on meaning and a secondary focus on form. This is in no way to say that grammar is unnecessary! Quite the contrary: one of the problems in the past with the extremes of the communicative approach was the lack of formalisation of what had been learnt, and this formalisation is important. Communication is not just about transactional language, but also about expressing feelings, needs, hopes, narrating experiences and arguing a point of view. None of this can be done without an ever firmer grammatical framework. Fortunately, the whole trend of contemporary approaches to teaching and learning is swinging back to a proper appreciation of the role of grammar.

Willis and Willis (2007, see "Further reading") call these two views "getting it right in the beginning" and "getting it right in the end".

Integrating grammar

Our position on this subject is clearly indicated by the book's central theme: *Learning by doing*. Whatever approach you use in teaching, students will retain structures better if they use them and work them out by themselves, with you in your roles as guide, expert, coach and facilitator. In this chapter we will explore different ways of integrating grammar into action.

Focus on form/structure can be divided into the following three broad categories, as given by Ellis (2003, see "Further reading").

- *Focus on forms*: pre-selected forms are presented to the student, either implicitly (inferring the rules from a set of exercises and through communicative activities exploiting the forms) or explicitly (structure-based instruction, teaching the rules). Often used as preparation for a task.

- *Planned focus on form*: treating pre-selected forms while the student is focused primarily on meaning (the text will contain the form, the activities call for that form to be used). Often used after the task, but also during it.

- *Incidental focus on form*: the form is not pre-selected and attention is drawn to it incidentally while the student is focused primarily on meaning. This might mean:
  - *recasts*, where the teacher or another student takes up the erroneous utterance and corrects it before feeding it back to the student speaking, a kind of implicit corrective feedback
  - *negotiation of meaning*, where what a student has said is not fully understood by the teacher or vice versa, and they engage in an exchange to find out what was meant. Students do try to make sense of what they hear, in any learning situation, and instances of such negotiation are frequent. An example may be where a word is unknown, and the teacher uses known words to explain the unknown during the task.

Incidental Focus on Form often occurs during the task but also after it.

Focus on form can be reactive, therefore, driven by the student's reaction to a task or to an input, or it can be pre-emptive, driven by the teacher.

Sounds, words and structures

In its Chapter 9, "Sounds, words and structures", the Report of the National Curriculum Working Group for Modern Foreign Languages (MFLWG) makes the distinction between:

a. practice (pre-communicative or reinforcing exercises)

b. performance (realistic and independent communication)

c. clarification (demonstration of how the model works).

It goes on: "The first is necessary, and the last may be very helpful, but the purpose of both is to promote better performance."[1]

"The distinction between structure and vocabulary is often quite artificial"[2]

Especially if vocabulary is learnt in phrases, many structures can be added to a student's stock of language long before they are dealt with systematically – this is part of element (a), "practice". For example, the conditional structure "I'd like . . ." is almost always taught very early, as vocabulary. Other good candidates for this treatment are noun–adjective phrases (word-order and agreement), questions, negative usages, modal verbs + infinitive, past tenses of common verbs, and common case usages.

Element (c), "clarification" of structures, may not itself be communicative, but it must always be closely linked to communication and support element (b), "performance".

The underlying model

Once they have thoroughly absorbed a set of related chunks of language, learners need to explore *and if necessary* be shown *how the underlying model works, not* be told *about it.*[3]

Possible steps on the path towards mastering the "underlying model" are as follows.

i. *First acquaintance.* You pick a structure that will be introduced soon and use it in familiar contexts and with known vocabulary, but without making a special point of it.

ii. *Memorisation.* The structure is included, with familiar vocabulary, in phrases and short sentences that students learn by heart.

iii. *Familiarisation.* Students use the learnt phrases and sentences in familiar contexts adapted to bring in the structure. For example, adjectives formerly used only as a predicate, as in *The book is red*, are used attributively with nouns to answer questions such as *What sort of book?* or *Which book?* – especially relevant to Germanic languages.

---

[1] MFLWG Report. §9.4 (i).
[2] Ibid. §9.3.
[3] Ibid. §9.4 (iv) (emphasis added).

iv. *Clarification through demonstration.* Students are shown the workings of the structure. This is done in stages, from a first outline to increasingly complete understanding. Wherever possible, support the demonstration visually, using pictures, diagrams or even just different colours in a text. This stage should always be combined with:

v. *Active response.* Students tackle a graduated series of tasks designed to show that they have grasped how the structure is used. In all these, it is very helpful to collaborate with a partner who checks the accuracy of the work – though you must confirm this.

vi. *Realistic use.* Students work on topics in which it is natural to use the phrases they've learnt. In this way they familiarise themselves with the structure.

vii. *Exploration.* Students summarise their understanding of a structure. This increases their sense of responsibility for their own learning, and allows you to identify and correct any misunderstandings. Students may not cope well with formal grammatical statements, but they can spot the difference between contrasting usages and say why they are different, or simply comment on the form/endings of given nouns, adjectives or verbs, etc.

viii. *Reinforcement.* Like vocabulary, structures need to be regularly "revisited", either through specific exercises or as a necessary part of a wider task.

Step vii can be inserted wherever appropriate – with some classes even before Step iv, and with all as part of Step viii.

Examples of exercises

In all activities, use *partners* as much as possible – A produces, passes to B/C, who answers, corrects, etc.

- Students underline the phrases that use the structure(s), perhaps varying the sort of line (single, double, wavy, dotted . . .) used to distinguish between different usages.

- They write passages on topics that force the use of the structure(s). For example, write a piece with both descriptions/ongoing actions and one-off actions in the past, then underline each verb in a different colour; write a description using both given adjectives and any others; etc.

- They copy/construct a diagram (for example, a time-line), list relevant phrases/structures under the correct heading, write sentences using them.

- "Pick-&-mix tables": students must construct grammatically correct (though possibly absurd) sentences from a table that has each part of speech or syntactical function in a different slot. (See boxed examples below, where a harder task, and greater possibility of error, can be made by jumbling up the entries in the subject and main verb columns.)

- You have a phrase in mind that the students have to predict. A student predicts. You indicate how many elements were incorrect, then another student starts again from the beginning. They will start to identify the correct elements until they settle on your chosen phrase.

- *Cloze* technique, in which the blanks all represent the structure. The missing words are usually not listed, because the emphasis is here on correct *form* – the meaning should be clear from the context, and any correct, meaningful answer is accepted. However, it is essential that students know the words needed. *Cloze* doesn't work so well if they cannot supply a suitable word.

- Students write any statements on structures contained in a given text, or write questions on structures for partners to answer. (Although this is not a thorough check on understanding, it encourages students to think about the role of structure in communication.)

- Students can teach each other grammar, e.g., by making "mind maps"/"structure webs" (see next).

- Examples of "thinking skills" covering both grammar and vocabulary:[4]

  o "odd one out" of a series of four/five words – several could be "odd", for different reasons
  o "concept maps": students draw lines between several given words, labelling the lines with what each pair has in common
  o "mind maps": generally a part of brainstorming, where the associations of a central idea are linked to it like the strands of a web (hence sometimes called "spider's web"); e.g., "holidays" or "work"
  o "structure webs": a format similar to a mind map, where the central focus is a structure and the branches lead to its possible uses; e.g., situations in which reflexive verbs might be used.

In all of these, students must justify their choice. With practice, they can suggest the words and ideas themselves – both good for their thinking skills and a great labour-saver for you.

---

[4] First two demonstrated by Phil Drabble and Claire Seccombe (Sunderland LEA) at a CILT conference, 16 November 2002.

Integrating grammar

Par exemple . . .   FORMEZ DES PHRASES ! . . .

Sujet		Verbe modal		Infinitif	Objet
Michel Sandrine Ma sœur Mon père	(ne)	veut peut doit va	(pas)	toucher manger regarder trouver ramasser embrasser	mon serpent. cette grenouille. les frites. nos poissons rouges. le petit éléphant. le grand gorille.
Jean et Alix Mes parents Mes frères Nos amis		veulent peuvent doivent vont			

Zum Beispiel . . .   BILDET SÄTZE! . . .

Vorfeld	Mittelfeld					Nachfeld
Mein Bruder Meine Schwester Meine Mutter Manfred	hat ist will kann hofft	oft lieber Sabine Siegfried meine Grosseltern	in die Stadt auf Urlaub alle Fenster dein Fahrrad eine Flasche Bier		(zu)	gegangen. gefahren. gehen. fahren. aufgemacht. gestohlen.
Gestern Nächste Woche Morgen Am Freitag	haben sind wollen	unsere Hunde nie leider	nach Hause zu Hause unsren Reisekoffer			kaufen. zumachen. geblieben. bleiben.
Meine Eltern Meine Freunde Meine Katzen Mia und Karl	müssen beginnen	wir jetzt am Wochenende	ihre Geschenke			kaufen.

Por ejemplo . . .   ¡FORMAD ORACIONES! . . .

Sujeto		Verbo principal	Infinitivo	(a+) artículo	Complemento
José Carmen Mi tía Nuestro perro	(no)	quiere puede tiene que va a	comprar hablar con entender encontrar tocar recoger ayudar buscar	a al a la a los a las el la los las	rata blanca. paella sabroso. profesor de física. libro pesado. bombero gordo. rana verde. camarera amable. chimpancé listo. guitarra cara.
Luis y Pilar Mis abuelos Tus niños Sus amigos		esperan deben pueden van a			

Task-based learning

Another way of looking at learning about the structures of the language uses the model mentioned in Chapter 19 on vocabulary learning: *notice the structure – understand how it works – acquire it*. The documents confronting students contain certain new structures, among others that they already know. This is not to say that the input needs to be flooded with the new structure. In fact, it is better if the new structure is used lightly in each document.

While working on understanding the documents, students are already beginning to notice the new structures. They may well take time out from studying the documents to ask you to help them to understand this new structure. This "time-out" can promote interlanguage restructuring on the students' part, i.e., they improve their comprehension of what they had previously only half understood. For instance, students of English (or small children) might have learnt that the past participle is verb+*ed*, and will apply that acquired rule to all verbs before slowly restructuring their interlanguage to include variants. The notion of a "comfort zone" is important here. The students are reassured if the tasks/activities are within their comfort zone, i.e., they can do them without difficulty, just slightly stretching their skills. Further than this, and they can do them with help. And this is where you come in.

In task-based learning, the focus on form comes in the pre-selection of the input. This may be:

- during the task, when the students are asked to reformulate what they have read, for example, or to draft a reply to something, or take part in an interaction
- in-task during a time-out period, when they turn for help to someone else
- post-task, when you draw the students' attention to the particular structure.

Simple tasks that involve the thinking skills of grammar and vocabulary include:

- asking students to guess what the form is before you focus on it. Alternatively, have them vote on what caused the most problems during the task. Ask for suggestions, put them on the board and ask the students to vote for the one they would like to work on. Then act on that.

- having students create the texts for their fellows. This could be done for lots of different scenarios, but it calls for a good level of accuracy and implies drafting and rewriting in the case of written texts, or rehearsal and planning in the case of aural texts

- encouraging reformulation by taking a long and complex sentence from the text, putting it up for display (OHP, presentation software, interactive whiteboard) and asking students to propose the rubbing out of one word at a time until the sentence no longer has any sense/is no longer grammatically correct

- alternatively, putting the same sort of sentence on display, after having taken out words that form part of the structure. Have the students suggest what the missing words are, and justify why they think so. By doing this they are making sense of how the structure works, having already understood the sentence

- using a skeleton of the text they have studied and having them reconstruct it. This can be from oral and textual input.

Embedding grammar in a context makes it feel more relevant and less as though the structure has been parachuted in out of the wide blue sky! Students sense that they have already seen it somewhere and are more receptive to focusing their attention on it. Engaging their cognitive skills will help them to construct meaning from this new world of language they are experiencing. That construction can become a co-construction with the help of other students and the teacher, a kind of collaborative grammar-learning project. As with many of the ideas in the preceding chapters, adapting them to your own context can involve creative solutions – who said grammar was boring?!

CHAPTER 21

Conclusion

Teaching modern foreign languages is a complex task, not made easier by the various waves, both political and academic, that have washed over it in recent years. The shift from a teacher-centred to a learner-centred and now to a learning-centred approach has had a major benefit: the last of these, unlike its two predecessors, does not imply a predominance of one side of teaching and learning over the other. Both you the teacher and your students are equally involved in the learning process: by the nature of it, they play the major role, but only you can structure their learning so that they have maximum opportunities to participate actively.

Another benefit of the learning-centred approach is, as we said in the first chapter, that it combines easily with whatever current objective your course may have: to strengthen oral skills, to enhance the understanding of grammatical structures, or to build up students' stock of words and phrases. It has been the principal aim of the book to enable you, whatever your emphasis, to engage your students to the maximum, and we hope you will find that it helps you to do so.

Further reading

NOTE: some of the works listed below, especially those formerly published by CILT, may no longer be in print, but the titles are included in case they are still available, either from book-sellers or in libraries.

Abbreviations: CB = CILT Briefings; IT = CILT InfoTech; PF = CILT Pathfinder; RF = CILT Resource File; RoP = CILT Reflections on practice.

General

Language Testing (journal published by SAGE).

Teaching learners how to learn. Strategy training in the modern languages classroom (Vee Harris, PF31).

Boys' performance in modern foreign languages. Listening to learners (Barry Jones, Gwynneth Jones, *et al.*, CILT).

Differentiation and individual learners. A guide to classroom practice (Anne Covery and Do Coyle, PF37).

Nightshift. Ideas and strategies for homework (David Buckland and Mike Short, PF20).

Researching pedagogic tasks Second language learning, teaching and testing (M. Bygate, P. Skehan and M. Swain, Pearson Education/Longman, Harlow, 2001).

Chapter 4

Assessment and planning in the MFL department (Harmer Parr, PF29).

Chapter 5

Reflections on the target language (Ed. Peter S. Neil, RoP4).

Up, up and away. Using classroom target language to help learners say what they want to say (Tony Elston, RF2).

Chapter 6

Dictation: New methods, new possibilities (P. Davis and M. Rinvolucri, Cambridge Handbooks for Language Teachers, 1988).

Chapter 8

Pairwork. Interaction in the modern languages classroom (Wendy Phillips, PF38).
Something to say? Promoting spontaneous classroom talk (Vee Harris, James Burch, Barry Jones and Jane Darcy, CILT).

Chapter 11

Seriously considering play: Designing interactive learning environments based on the blending of microworlds, simulations, and games. (L. P. Rieber, *Educational Technology Research & Development*, 44(2), 43–58, 1996).
Maximizing the benefits of project work in foreign language classrooms (Bülent Alan and Fredricka L. Stoller, in *Forum*, a Journal for the Teachers of English, Vol. 43, 2005).
Task-based language learning and teaching (R. Ellis, OUP, 2003).
Two ways of defining communication strategies (C. Faerch and G. Kaspar, in *Language Learning*, 34, 1984).
Promoting self-regulation in the development of speaking proficiency in Spanish (Peggy Buckwalter, in *Vida Hispánica*, ALL, Autumn 2007, p9).

Chapter 15

More reading for pleasure in a foreign language (Ann Swarbrick, PF36).
Reflections on reading. From GCSE to A-level (Ed. Mike Grenfell, RoP2).

Chapter 16

Once upon a time: Using stories in the language classroom (John Morgan, Mario Rinvolucri, Cambridge University Press, 1983).

Chapter 17

Just write (Julie Adams and Sally Ann Panter, PF40).

Chapter 18

Making effective use of the dictionary (Gwen Berwick and Gwen Horsfall, PF28).

Chapter 19

Words – Teaching and learning vocabulary (David Snow, PF34).

Task-based interaction and incidental vocabulary learning: A case study (J. Newton, *in Second Language Research*, 1995, 11, 2: 159–177 [13.2]).

Doing task-based teaching (D. Willis and J. Willis, OUP, 2007).

Task-based language learning and teaching (R. Ellis, OUP, 2003).

Chapter 20

Reflections on grammar-implicit teaching (Margaret Wells, RoP5).

Stimulating grammatical awareness. A fresh look at language acquisition (Heather Rendall, PF33).

A cognitive approach to language learning (P. Skehan, OUP, 1998).

Index

Index